YOUR
CHILD
& THE
NEW
AGE

D1367825

Enemy-occupied territory—that is what this world is. Christianity is the story of how the rightful king has landed, you might say landed in disguise, and is calling us all to take part in a great campaign of sabotage....

Now, today, this moment, is our great chance to choose the right side. God is holding back to give us that chance. It will not last forever. We must take it or leave it.

C.S. Lewis, *Mere Christianity*

YOUR CHILD & THE NEW AGE

BERIT KJOS

VICTOR BOOKS®

A DIVISION OF SCRIPTURE PRESS PUBLICATIONS INC.
USA CANADA ENGLAND

Unless otherwise noted, Scripture quotations are from the *Holy Bible, New International Version*, © 1973, 1978, 1984, International Bible Society. Used by permission of Zondervan Bible Publishers. Other quotations are from the *King James Version* (KJV) and *The New Testament in Modern English* (PH), © by J.B. Phillips, 1958, 1960, 1972, permission of Macmillan Publishing Co. and Collins Publishers.

2   3   4   5   6   7   8   9   10   Printing/Year   94   93   92   91   90

Library of Congress Cataloging-in-Publication Data

Kjos, Berit.
    Your Child and the New Age / by Berit Kjos.
        p.   cm.
    Includes bibliographical references.
    ISBN 0-89693-795-X   :
    1. New Age movement—Controversial literature. 2. United States—Moral conditions. 3. Parenting—Religious aspects —Christianity.

I. Title.
BP605.N48K57   1990
248.8′45—dc20
                                                        89-48595
                                                        CIP

© 1990 by SP Publications, Inc. All rights reserved
Printed in the United States of America

No part of this book may be reproduced without written permission except for brief quotations in books and critical reviews. For information, write Victor Books, Wheaton, Illinois 60187

CONTENTS

PREFACE

Tempting voices beckon to children everywhere. Schools, movies, music, and books all sound the camouflaged call of the serpent: "Come, dream, wield the Force, trust Self, be God, create your own reality, build a new world. Anything goes, for sin and guilt exist only in the minds of the religious."

How can we help our children *to say no?*

God points us to His answer: "My people are destroyed from lack of knowledge" (Hosea 4:6). We can teach our children to know Truth, so that they will discern the counterfeit. And we can tell them about New Age enticements, so that they will choose not to experience them.

The purpose of this book is to expose New Age deception and to equip families to stand together in confident, loving resistance. It is *not* to condemn schools or media presentations. Countless wonderful teachers continue to bring good values to the classroom. Many books, movies, and television programs still reflect Judeo/Christian thinking.

However, New Age thought and practices have entered the schools and the media to such an extent that none of our children are immune. While counterfeit spirituality may find more fertile ground in certain schools, it colors textbooks, television, and toys nationwide. It defies opposition, because it usually *sounds* good. Tailor-made to fit their human nature and western culture, it offers whatever children want to hear, see, have, and be.

Brooks Alexander, founder of Spiritual Counterfeits

Project, exposed the heart of New Age deception in a 1983 SPC report, *The Coming World Religion:*

> *Evil is not the opposite of good, as though it might co-exist on an equal basis. Evil is a distortion of the goodness God created. . . .*
>
> *Evil, the Bible shows us, is . . . an ontological parasite. It rides on the back of the given good, even as it deforms it. For that reason, it is never evil in itself that tempts us. It is always a good that attracts us—on that we imagine, an even "better" good than that which God proposes. . . .*
>
> *At its heart, the lie is seduction to an idolatry of the image of God, a worship of the self and its powers, disguised as "secret knowledge" and presented as "god-realization."*

Confident that God reigns, we can confront these deceptive forces which reach out for children's hearts and minds. He, who loves our children even more than we do, will show us how to prepare them to recognize and resist evil—no matter how inviting its call.

"Thanks be to God! He gives us the victory through our Lord Jesus Christ" (1 Corinthians 15:57).

Berit Kjos
Los Altos, California
1990

A PARABLE

High on a ridge overlooking the valley stood the King, framed in the sun's fading light. His form rose like a monument of unyielding strength. Above his head swirled hostile, black clouds. Raging winds snatched at his coat. Yet, he who could quell their assault with a word refused to be distracted. He had fixed his eyes on the valley below. Capturing each tiny detail, he traced the movement of gathering armies. Suddenly his gaze rested on a shadowy form well hidden from ordinary sight. Anger and agony flashed across his noble face.

"Once I cherished that imposter," he mused, "but the Prince of Darkness only loved himself. I made him strong and beautiful, but he used my gifts to build his own throne. Did he imagine that his mutinous force could quench my power and hinder my plan? Has he spoken his own lies so often that he has deceived himself as well as my people? His foolish pride kindled this war, but soon even his blinded slaves will see the triumph of my kingdom."

The King's focus moved from the enemy headquarters to the city nearby. Its people slept unconcerned, smug, oblivious to the scheming, waiting legions.

Tears stung the King's eyes as he spoke to the city he loved. "If only you had listened," he whispered softly. "If only you knew. . . . But you ignored my warnings and went your own way. You listened only to comfortable words that fit your selfish dreams—lies and false promises that were more pleasant to your ears than my truth.

"My foolish people, open your eyes and see. I came to love and care for you, but you turned away. The thief came to steal and destroy, and you worship him. If you only knew where you are heading. . . ."

Far below, near the edge of the city, where the forest opened to a wide clearing, the grim armies merged into a ghostly, quaking mass. Suddenly, without a sound, a message burst into their consciousness: The prince has arrived. As one, they bowed in fearful surrender, breathing their salute: "Hail, Prince of Darkness! Master of the Force! Hail!"

Before them rose the tall, dark figure of the prince. "My friends," he purred, "I hear you have done well!"

A wave of relief swept over the mass.

"Report your progress!" his voice cracked like a whip over shivering slaves. "Have you captured the city? Are its people ready to follow?"

Silence hung like an ominous sword over the trembling warriors. Brash tyrants away from their master, they cowered like frightened dogs in his presence. Finally a creature stepped forward. "Sir, the coup is almost complete. The city has yielded to your control."

"How did you win their allegiance?" demanded the prince.

"We followed your plan, Sir. You told us to target the children. To reform their schools, pollute their movies . . .

"Stop, stop! I want details. Who handled the schools?"

"I did, Sir." A burly figure lumbered to the front line. Under the heavy cowl which hid his features, his body was shaking.

"Explain your strategy."

"We followed our ancient plan, Sir. You told us to change labels to fit contemporary tastes—and it worked. First we whispered doubts about the King's repulsive book of truth. Then we planted tantalizing visions of the New World into the minds of educators. We showed them irresistible images of their divinity, the power of

Self, the pleasures of sex, and the peace of global unity under your mighty reign.

"Slow down and describe their response."

"Those who were open to transformation were thrilled with their new discoveries. They quickly fit your ideas into their curriculum."

"Is that all?"

"No, there's much more! We also told them that the King's values hinder the freedom, growth, and happiness of Self. To build a better world, they must discard obsolete boundaries and pave new paths to higher consciousness and spiritual oneness. Quick to catch on, the kids are learning to ridicule the King's archaic standards and narrow-minded subjects. Soon they'll hate all who oppose your plan!" He giggled.

"Well done," grimaced the prince, "but control yourself."

Scanning the dark mass, he shouted, "Who's in charge of music?"

A squat, slinking creature crept forward. "I am, Sir."

"Report your progress!"

"We have revived your fool-proof formula: drums, drugs, and sensual delights. This formula blocks reason and keeps our connections open. We give them a good time—and make sure they come back for more. With more advanced subjects, we no longer hide your identity. They crave your savage malevolence."

"Well done!" The prince rubbed his hands in obvious glee before he shouted, "Next! Who transformed television?"

"We did," answered a shrill voice. A short, stocky figure pushed his way to the front. "One battalion loaded cartoons with wizards and superheroes winning battles by your cosmic energy. Kids want supernatural power, so we've showed them yours. Camouflaged, of course."

"Splendid!" The prince's cruel voice rose excitedly. "Soon they'll want more, and when they're hooked, they too will be glad to see me. Ha! I will be their god, and they will learn a new form of worship! Go on. Tell me more."

"We have been showing our vision for the new world order to reporters, producers, and writers." He snickered. "We convinced them that the King's values block progress. Today children choose their own way—or rather, our way . . ."

"*My* way, you mean!" shrieked the prince.

"Your way, Sir!" quaked the commander.

"You met no resistance?"

"Not much. Your brilliant ideas usually excite them."

"What about the King's subjects?"

"Many don't notice. Since we keep them too busy to study the Book of Truth, they can't tell your plan from the King's. Some are afraid to speak up. The fools who complain face our correction squad. Ridicule and exclusion usually silence them." Cheers rose in agreement.

For a moment, the prince gazed silently into that dark mass of veiled warriors. Fear and hatred, not love and loyalty, bound these miserable subjects to do his bidding.

"Watch every rebellious subject!" he shouted. "Find loopholes in their armor. Distract those who pray. And above all, hinder their use of the Book."

Lightning slashed the sky and the distant thunder grew to a deafening roar. But the King kept his watchful position high above the city, waiting for the precise moment . . .

Suddenly he raised his right arm. "Be still," he cried into the storm. And the storm stilled around the summit.

He raised his left arm, and a battalion of soldiers dressed in white appeared before him.

"It is time! I have awakened my remnant. I have spoken to all who have ears to hear and eyes to see. To everyone not blinded and bound by deception. To those who have not bowed to the Prince of Darkness.

"I have told them to rise, take their swords, and fight for their families and children. You must take your positions at their sides. Sing with them the song of victory, then conquer the forces of evil in the name of the King."

PART ONE

SCHOOLS

CHAPTER ONE
Schools and Counterfeit Spirituality

*'Tis education forms the common mind:
just as the twig is bent the tree's inclined. (Alexander Pope)*

*This nation has been targeted for a massive takeover. While our
military experts are concentrating on bombs and missiles, a different kind of battle is being waged for America's heart and
soul . . . a battle between two supernatural beings who seek the
devotion of men. (Erwin W. Lutzer and John F. DeVries,* Satan's
"Evangelistic" Strategy for This New Age*)*

A fifth-grade teacher in Lakewood, Colorado placed a wide
assortment of books in his classroom for students to enjoy
during daily reading times. When a parent complained that
two of the 239 volumes were based on the Bible, the principal told teacher Ken Roberts to remove them.

On January 5, 1989 a judge upheld the school's order to
censor the two books from the classroom. In school the
children could legally read books on Buddhism, Indian religions, and Greek mythology—but not on Christianity.[1]

In October 1988, 300 teachers and school employees in
San Jose, California gathered to "improve education" with
workshops and lectures on communication, relaxation, and
self-esteem. One group sat cross-legged in a darkened
classroom, learning how to reduce stress with yoga. While
some felt self-conscious, others happily released their
minds to the quieting sounds that flowed from a tape play-
er on the desk. In the next room, another group meditated
behind locked doors.[2]

Tens of thousands of classroom teachers, educational consultants and psychologists, counselors, administrators . . . have been among the millions engaged in *personal transformation.* They have only recently begun to link . . . to share strategies. (Marilyn Ferguson, *The Aquarian Conspiracy*)

In another California town, a third-grader pressed his fingers against his temples, shut his eyes tight, and wrinkled his face in intense concentration. He was trying to "read" the symbols touched by the teacher's assistant seated on the other side of a large partition. On the reading instructor's desk lay a book titled *ESP.*[3]

Masks of the New Age

The New Age is actually ancient occultism with a facelift. It is the beautiful side of evil, an enticing facade for the kingdom of darkness. Disguised as peace, power, wisdom, and love, this attractive deception pretends to offer everything God promises, yet asks nothing in return—for the moment. Its seductive call to "be like God" dates back to the Garden of Eden. God warned us long ago about deceptions which would lead many to "abandon the faith and follow deceiving spirits and things taught by demons" (1 Timothy 4:1).

For the time will come when men will not put up with sound doctrine. Instead, to suit their own desires, they will gather around them a great number of teachers to say what their itching ears want to hear. They will turn their ears away from the truth and turn aside to myths. (2 Timothy 4:3-5)

Today's most popular myth distorts the character of God and the identity of man. Unwilling to bow to a personal, sovereign God, multitudes have reshaped their Creator into an image of their own wishful thinking. This imagined god becomes an impersonal power source ready to fulfill the whims of a god-man determined to direct his own destiny.

The New Age shuns Christianity but welcomes all other religions. Each person adjusts what he already believes, adds the desired ingredients, and finds himself immersed in the counterfeit. Almost any combination works:

☐ Humanism plus supernatural power becomes New Age

☐ Hinduism plus pop psychology becomes New Age

☐ Pantheism plus confidence in human potential becomes New Age

☐ Even "crossless Christianity" fits, if we subtract its heart—Jesus Christ and His atonement—and then add some Eastern mysticism.

The New Age is "a smorgasbord of spiritual substitutes for Christianity, all heralding our unlimited potential to transform ourselves and the planet so that a 'New Age' of peace, light and love will break forth." (Doug Groothuis, "Confronting the New Age Counterfeit")

In spite of grandiose claims by New Age leaders and the effective networking among New Age groups, we cannot give them all the credit for the phenomenal spread of this deception. That belongs to the mastermind behind the scenes, the "god of forces." Satan has a brilliant plan and whispers or channels portions of it to any who will listen— anywhere in the world. He intends to set up global government in which he will reign unopposed through his puppet, the Antichrist. To win, he needs to recruit more soldiers. Our children are among those he has targeted.

Satan can counterfeit many of the good things God gives us. In his hands, even tools for learning can become weapons loaded with distorted messages aimed at young minds. Look at his three major thrusts toward global society:

☐ Replace biblical Christianity with a *self*-centered blend of *all religions* joined in spiritual oneness.

☐ Replace Judeo/Christian values with New Age values—anything that frees a person to follow the desires of self and create his own reality.

□ Replace nationalism with a one-world government under a spiritually evolved leadership.

War on Christianity

Humanism paved the way for the New Age, but most of us didn't notice. Just as termites can chew away at a home's foundations for decades before the damage shows, so humanist educators have sought to undermine the public school system. Suddenly we had to face the fact that many schools teach goals and values that contradict God's. And that the humanist-oriented educational establishment promotes its beliefs as aggressively as any other religious group. Listen to their war cry:

> *The battle for humankind's future must be waged and won in the public school classroom by teachers who correctly perceive their role as the proselytizers of a new faith: a religion of humanity that recognizes and respects the spark of what theologians call divinity in every human being.*
>
> *These teachers must embody the same selfless dedication as the most rabid fundamentalist preachers, for they will be ministers of another sort, utilizing a classroom instead of a pulpit to convey humanist values in whatever subject they teach, regardless of the educational level—preschool, day care, or large state university.*
>
> *The classroom must and will become an arena of conflict between the old and the new—the rotting corpse of Christianity, together with all its adjacent evils and misery, and the new faith of humanism, resplendent in its promise of a world in which the never-realized Christian ideal of "love thy neighbor" will finally be achieved.*[4]

American philosopher and educator John Dewey kindled the fire of educational reform. The first president of the American Humanist Association, Dewey was determined to weed out Christian absolutes and reseed with "truths" that could adjust to changing cultures. The *Humanist Manifesto* which Dewey signed in 1933 declares the heart of the movement. This is part of its introduction:

There is great danger of a final, and we believe fatal, identification of the word religion with doctrines and methods which have lost their significance and which are powerless to solve the problem of human living in the Twentieth Century. . . . Any religion that can hope to be a synthesizing and dynamic force for today, must be shaped for the needs of this age. To establish such a religion is a major necessity of the present.[5]

Secular Humanists Believe:	*Christians Believe:*
There is no God.	We trust in a living, personal God.
The world is self-existing.	God created the world.
Everything "exists for the fulfillment of human life."	"From Him and through Him and to Him are all things." Romans 11:36
"The goal . . . is a free and universal society" where "people cooperate for common good."	Our goal is to "know" Christ and the "power of His resurrection." Philippians 3:10
"Man is responsible for the realization . . . of his dreams."	"My salvation and my honor depend on God." Psalm 62:7
Values are relative and changing, determined by human need.	Biblical values are absolute and unchanging. Matthew 24:35
Man has within himself the power to create a new world.	"What is impossible with men is possible with God." Luke 18:27

Without the National Education Association, called "the

nation's most powerful political machine," Dewey's ideas might have been confined to university campuses. Supported by the NEA, comprised of textbook writers and superintendents as well as professors and public school teachers, Dewey's vision spread like wildfire. Through its militant leadership, the whole educational system became involved—with or without the personal support of local educators, many of whom didn't realize what was happening.

Few textbooks escaped the watchful eye of NEA censors, who doggedly followed Dewey's plan to provide a "purified environment for the child." Historical facts that clashed with "progressive education" were distorted or erased. The NEA seeks total control of curriculum content, control of teachers' colleges, and sex education free from parental interference. Though seventy-five percent of American teachers consider themselves "moderate or conservative," the NEA supports abortion on demand (without parental consent), preferential treatment of homosexuals, and unilateral nuclear freeze.[6]

Professor Paul Vitz's book, *Censorship: Evidence of Bias in Our Children's Textbooks*, unveiled some alarming facts. Christianity, family values, and certain political and economic positions have been systematically banished from children's textbooks. For example, in 670 stories from third- and sixth-grade readers:

□ "No story features Christian or Jewish religious motivation, although one story does make American Indian religion the central theme in the life of a white girl. . . ."

□ "Almost no story features marriage or motherhood as important or positive. . . . But there are many aggressively feminist stories that openly deride manhood. . . ."

□ In an original story by Isaac Bashevis Singer, the main character prayed "to God" and later remarked "Thank God." In the story as presented in the sixth-grade reader, the words "to God" were taken out and the expression "Thank God" was changed to "Thank goodness."

While some elementary social studies textbooks told about Thanksgiving, they did not explain to whom the Pilgrims gave thanks. Pilgrims were defined as "people who make long trips." The Pueblo Indians "can pray to Mother Earth—but Pilgrims can't be described as praying to God."[7]

Overt attacks on Christianity through distortion, depreciation, and ridicule cause more damage than omissions. Many of the books students are required to read refer to boring church services, self-righteous ministers, and lustful evangelists. One psychology text equated the historical Jesus with mythological gods: "A great many myths deal with the idea of rebirth. Jesus, Dionysus, Odin, and many other traditional figures are represented as having died, after which they were reborn, or arose from the dead."[8]

What happens when children are subjected to such suggestions and pressures year after year? Many yield to the hostile forces that oppose their beliefs. But God stands ready each moment to provide wisdom and strength to match the challenge. He longs to show us how to fight and win each spiritual battle. Therefore He reminds us:

> *You, dear children, are from God and have overcome them, because the One who is in you is greater than the one who is in the world. They are from the world and therefore speak from the viewpoint of the world, and the world listens to them. We are from God, and whoever knows God listens to us; but whoever is not from God does not listen to us. This is how we recognize the Spirit of truth and the spirit of falsehood. (1 John 4:4-6)*

Embracing Eastern Mysticism

Though religious in fervor and commitment, humanism failed to meet man's spiritual needs. As the front door of the school closed to God, the back door swung wide open to New Age teaching. Disguised as stress reduction, relaxation, centering, or transpersonal education—or just tucked unnamed into a traditional curriculum—it added spiritual power to the existing man-centered program.

Few educators resisted the "positive" new approaches to learning and "wholeness." The counterfeit god, (the Source, Force, Cosmic Consciousness, Universal Mind, Self), satisfied anti-Christian humanists, well-meaning

One of the biggest advantages we have as New Agers is, once the occult, metaphysical and New Age terminology is removed, we have concepts and techniques that are very acceptable to the general public. So we can change the names . . . demonstrate the power [and] open the door to millions who normally would not be receptive. (New Age leader, Dick Sutphen, in an article entitled "Infiltrating the New Age into Society")

teachers, and adventurous children. And it completed the lie. Humanist selfism added to New Age spirituality formed a plausible picture of reality—one that fit human nature and sanctioned the trappings of old-time paganism.

Paganism? You mean drums, sensuality, orgies, and witchcraft? Right. However, the New Age preferred to hide its dark, sinister side until it had popularized its light, appealing side. Introduced in disarmingly noble and affirming terms, the counterfeit fooled all but those who had studied the genuine. Notice its enticing similarities to biblical truth, as well as its striking contradictions.

The Counterfeit	Biblical Truth	And God Also Says . . .
1. All is one: No distinction between God and man (Monism). God and Satan are merely two sides of the unified whole.	"There is neither Jew nor Greek, slave nor free, male nor female, for you are all one in Christ Jesus." Galatians 3:28	"You shall have no other gods before Me" Exodus 20:3. "Every knee will bow to Me, and every tongue will confess to God." Romans 14:11
2. All is god. God is an impersonal force flowing through each person, animal, plant, or thing (pantheism, but can easily appear as polytheism).	"Since the creation of the world God's invisible qualities—His eternal power and divine nature—have been clearly seen, being understood from what has been made." Romans 1:20	"They exchanged the truth of God for a lie, and worshiped and served created things rather than the Creator—who is forever praised." Romans 1:25

3. Man is god. God dwells in each person as his inner Self, a divine Source of all wisdom and power.	"I have been crucified with Christ and I no longer live, but Christ lives in me." Galatians 2:20	"This is what the Lord says. . . . 'I am the Lord, and there is no other.'" Isaiah 45:1, 5
4. Through changed consciousness, man evolves spiritually, gains awareness of his divine identity, and reaches self-realization.	"Do not conform any longer to the pattern of this world, but be transformed by the renewing of your mind." Romans 12:2	"In later times some will abandon the faith and follow deceiving spirits and things taught by demons." 1 Timothy 4:1
5. All religions are one. If any (like Christianity) is exclusive and refuses to agree, it commits the sin of separatism.	"I have given them the glory that You gave Me, that they may be one as We are one: I in them and You in Me." John 17:22-23	"Do not be yoked together with unbelievers. . . . What does a believer have in common with an unbeliever? . . . For we are the temple of the living God. . . . Therefore come out from them and be separate." 2 Corinthians 6:14-17
6. Cosmic evolution requires faith (such as: "the force is with us") and the spiritual participation of enough people to create a "critical mass."	"According to your faith will it be done to you" Matthew 9:29. "May they be brought to complete unity." John 17:23	"Salvation is found in no one else, for there is no other name under heaven given to men by which we must be saved." Acts 4:12
7. A new world order (globalism) requires a one world government, ruler, religion, and economy.	"From Him the whole body, joined and held together by every supporting ligament, grows and builds itself up in love, as each part does its work." Ephesians 4:16	"He also forced everyone . . . to receive a mark on his right hand or on his forehead, so that no one could buy or sell unless he had the mark. . . . His number is 666." Revelation 13:16, 18

Many American classrooms have become workshops where children can learn and practice New Age precepts. While some well-meaning teachers turn to meditation and guided imagery just because "it works," others base their actions on personal faith in New Age doctrines. Those who believe in oneness with the cosmic source of peace, wisdom, and creativity see an obvious way to help their students: Connect them to the Source!

Some teachers who forbid prayer to Jesus Christ in their classrooms see nothing wrong with Hindu-based meditational exercises that connect young minds with other gods.

Deborah Rozman trains teachers. An educational consultant and a transpersonal psychology instructor, she has written a teaching manual titled *Meditating with Children.* In her book, she thanks "the Universal Mother of Compassion found in all of nature . . . and Paramahansa Yogananda." She dedicates the book to "all children, everywhere, that they may evolve towards their spiritual destiny."[9]

Rozman's meditations delight teachers, quiet children, and invoke a dangerous spiritual force. Consider this drill. The children sit cross-legged in a circle on the floor and discuss the nature of spiritual energy. They straighten their backs so the "energy from the Source within can flow up . . . our spine into our brain."[10] The teacher then is supposed to lead the children in a visualization exercise. One begins: "Sitting very still with eyes closed . . . imagine that you are floating out of your spiritual eye (the point between the eyebrows) and into the leaf of the plant . . . feel the oneness of the source of all life everywhere. . . ."[11]

Or she may use this visualization: "Meditate and go into the Source within, and in that One Source feel that you are One with everyone else's Light, Intelligence, Love, and Power. . . . Chant 'Om' softly to fill the whole circle and the whole room with your experience of the Source within."[12]

The final step invites the children to extend their arms and be channels "for healing energy from the Source through you to another." The teacher tells the children to "feel energy traveling from the Center within down the arm and out . . . into the object or person." She explains that this is a way they "can help each other feel better."[13]

With each session, the children risk taking another step toward spiritual bondage. Few teachers realize that any contact with the occult can open the door to demonic strongholds and oppression. Invoking spiritual forces and channeling their power usually results in blindness to God, and a wide range of oppressive personality changes.

"Since New Age visualization techniques are identical to the techniques used by spiritualists to contact demons, the unwary initiate ends up suffering from much more than what any human power is able to deliver him from." (Paul Bartz, editor, Bible-Science Newsletter)

Stephanie Herzog first heard Ms. Rozman speak about meditation at a school district in-service meeting. Impressed, she began using meditation in her own classroom the next day. To avoid criticism from parents, she called it "centering" and "concentrating our energies."[14]

After years of unhindered classroom meditation, Ms. Herzog wrote her own book promoting these spiritual exercises. Its title, *Joy in the Classroom*, illustrates the appeal of New Age deception. She claims that the student can find joy, peace, wisdom, and strength (the counterfeit of God's promises) by enjoyable, seductive exercises that raise his consciousness and connect him with his true God-Self.

Such programs may be called confluent or wholistic education, transpersonal psychology, affective education, and accelerated learning. They are usually presented as stress management, suicide prevention, or self-esteem programs.

In addition to the possibility of occult bondage, children face a subtle challenge to their faith. If they learn that their God-given imagination can produce the reality they desire, why follow Jesus Christ? If pleasant meditations can connect them with the cosmic god, why choose the Cross? Their spiritual needs are being met — so it seems.

This inoculation against Christianity, together with the dangers of overt occult practices, calls parents to action. We need to know what schools are teaching our children. Dr. Shirley Correll, herself an educator, shares our concern about the newer forms of education. She describes a program called Quieting Reflex and Success Imagery:

> *Trusting children are psychologically manipulated into involvement with spirit guides, Eastern religion, hypnosis, altered states of consciousness, and occult activities forbidden to Christians.*
>
> *In one case, a little girl refused to pray in the name of Jesus after her imaginary wise person, or spirit guide, directed her not to. Children are often subtly conditioned not to discuss these programs with their parents, and some children are reluctant to admit the programs' existence.*[15]

Many textbooks, while silent on the subject of Christianity, don't hesitate to teach Buddhism and Hinduism. A World Cultures text even told students to pretend for several days that they were Hindus.[16] A Health Guidance text devoted several pages to the process and benefits of Eastern meditation. Picturing a teenage girl in Yoga position, it defined meditation as "a technique used to alter the states of consciousness and trigger relaxation response."[17]

A high school speech teacher in Mountain View, California told his students to give impromptu talks on the topic, "What I want to be in my next life."[18] Did he assume that reincarnation is now generally accepted among the youth?

This embrace of spiritual propaganda reaches beyond the bright side of the New Age. Defiantly challenging the patience of God and the cruel power of Satan, many schools dare welcome even the dark occult. In their informative book, *What Are They Teaching Our Children?*, Mel and Norma Gabler tell about a "witch license application" they discovered in a sixth-grade skills handbook. It first described the bizarre behavior of witches, then asked: "Suppose that you wanted to pursue a career as a witch. These days you might have to apply for a license and perhaps even join a witches' union. In any case, by filling out an application your aptitude for witchcraft could be evaluated." With the application came questions such as, "What words would you use to cast a spell?" and "What is your favorite formula for a witches' brew?"

Most students wouldn't have to search far to find answers. One thirteen-year-old boy shocked his uncle, who happened to be an ex-warlock, by showing him a book titled *Curses, Hexes and Spells.* Filled with detailed incantations and "everyday curses," it came from the Gladewater, Texas Middle School library.[19]

An increasing number of schools are telling students to research the occult, to role-play occult fantasy games such as Dungeons and Dragons, and to seek esoteric knowledge through horoscopes, I Ching, and Ouija boards. Needless to say, the children are playing with an incredible fire that neither they nor their teachers can control.

> *The coming of the lawless one will be in accordance with the work of Satan displayed in all kinds of counterfeit miracles, signs, and wonders, and in every sort of evil that deceives those who are perishing. They perish because they refused to love the truth and so be saved." (2 Thessalonians 2:9-12)*

Victory begins with knowing and loving God and His truth. From the living Word, our children will learn *genuine* wisdom, discern evil, conquer giants, walk in peace, and experience God's freedom!

CHAPTER TWO
What Can Parents Do About Counterfeit Spirituality?

Our struggle is not against flesh and blood, but against the rulers, against the authorities, against the powers of this dark world and against the spiritual forces of evil in the heavenly realms. (Ephesians 6:12)

The home has been ordained of God to prepare children for their inevitable encounter with a world that is often hostile to every godly principle we hold valid and precious, but also sometimes hungry for reality and truth. (Ethel Herr, Schools: How Parents Can Make a Difference*)*

Having seen the conflict, let's take a look at the invisible war behind the visible facts. Remember that the battle is infinitely greater than any potential conflict between your child and his school. Teachers and principals, many of whom share your values, *are not the enemy.* Neither are the humanist missionaries in the NEA. The real enemy is the one who opposed God's plan from the beginning. Satan uses his blinded victims to carry out his schemes.

Though the spiritual war grows fiercer around us, this is not a time to fear, despair, get angry, or lose hope. History has proven that times of ease and acceptance produce complacency, while repression and persecution produce strong, unified Christians. The battle's sudden visibility means that we can no longer ignore it. Nor can we fight this giant on our own.

God is our strength in this struggle against a counterfeit force. He *will* accomplish His purpose of maturing and uniting us in Him if we choose to stand together, seek His mighty resources, and follow His guidelines.

Nehemiah faced a battle similar to ours. When Satan sent human agents to mock, ridicule, incapacitate, and destroy God's people, Nehemiah prayed. God answered with a fool-proof plan that also works for us today:

Nehemiah	Christian Parents
1. They "prayed . . . and posted guard day and night." (Nehemiah 4:9)	"Put on the full armor of God. . . . Be alert and always keep on praying." Ephesians 6:11-18
2. They stationed families to stand guard together. (4:13)	As a family, teach and discuss truth, help each other resist deception.
3. They carried their weapons continually. (4:13, 16-18)	Know God's Word— your spiritual weapon.
4. At the sound of the trumpet, they joined together. (4:20)	Christian families— stand, pray, and fight deception together.

Step One: "Be Alert and Always Keep on Praying"

The battle begins and ends with prayer. Pray for open and trusting communication with your child. Pray for discernment to detect teaching that contradicts God's truth. Pray for wisdom to know when to speak up and what to say.

☐ Pray for your child. Pray that he learns to discern error on his own. Pray that he will be bold to speak truth, and will have the courage to stand alone when all his friends follow another god. Pray that pleasing God will be more important than pleasing teachers and peers.

☐ Pray together as a family. Put on the "full armor of God" daily. Remember that to "put on the belt of truth" means more than merely declaring it done. It means reading (or hearing) and following the Word, and knowing it well enough to discern error. Read and discuss Ephesians 6:13-17. Memorize the parts of the armor.

☐ Pray for oneness with other Christians. Pray for faithful Christian friends for your child. Pray for other parents who will stand with you. Since you see the need to get involved in your child's schooling, pray for direction.

☐ Pray for the school, for teachers, principals, counselors, the curriculum committee, and the school board. Pray that they learn God's truth, discern deception, choose the best curriculum, and make wise decisions.

"Do not be anxious about anything, but in everything, by prayer and petition, with thanksgiving, present your requests to God" (Philippians 4:6).

Step Two: Know What Your Child Is Learning in School

☐ Talk with your child. Listen for clues that help you spot good as well as questionable teaching. Be objective and model appreciation of schools and teachers.

Perhaps you have a child who gladly gives detailed accounts of all events from the time he left for school that morning. My boys preferred to answer all my questions with a brief "Good!" or "Okay." But I discovered that a tasty snack after school could produce at least five minutes of sharing. And today, a sandwich at a local deli with my fourteen-year-old boosts our conversations immensely.

I also found that communication mysteriously wilted when my sons suspected that my motive was cross-examination rather than having fun together, or if I kept so busy at home that I couldn't stop and listen.

If you and your child have been too busy to really listen to each other, it is not too late to begin now. Don't start by asking a lot of questions about school. Especially if he is a teenager. He probably won't be ready to share openly until he knows he can count on your empathetic response, non-judgmental attitude, and genuine interest in him. If he has found that his sharing produces anxiety, agitation, anger, and an impulsive trip to his teacher, he will probably hide all questionable information. No child wants to be an accomplice to an emotional or embarrassing confrontation.

☐ Volunteer to assist the teacher in the classroom. You will gain firsthand knowledge as well as easy access to the teacher's listening ear.

☐ Scan elementary textbooks, take-home papers, and fliers. Check to see if significant facts are deleted or distorted. Consider their effects on your child. Ask yourself the following questions about the above material:

–Does it censor out important facts about the influences of Christianity in the development of our country? Does it imply that Christianity is unimportant, old-fashioned, or a hindrance to progress? Does it ask your child to admit and discuss his faith in front of the class—thus leaving him open to embarrassment and ridicule? With new proposals for bringing religion back in schools, look carefully at the kinds and ways this religion will be taught. It could mean wide open doors to more counterfeits.

–Does it present an imbalanced view of Christians? Are pastors, evangelists, missionaries, and other Christians cheapened and ridiculed—never described favorably?

–Does it emphasize, promote, or give detailed descriptions of other religions, while ignoring Christianity?

–Does it require your child's participation in spiritual exercises? Does it give instructions in yoga, meditation, channeling, or guided imagery? Does it give practical instructions in the doctrines or techniques of other religions—such as Hinduism or Buddhism? Does it involve your child in research on occult activities?

–Does it ask your child not to share information with his parents?

☐ Discuss your findings with your child. Express your appreciation for the good things you see. Explain any area of concern. Teach discernment by pointing out contradictions to God's truth.

Step Three: Know and Exercise Your Privileges as a Parent

If you suspect a problem, you may need to talk with the teacher and, if necessary, ask to see the teacher's manual and classroom projects. But first . . .

☐ Discuss your plan with your child, if his age and understanding permit. Explain that God made you, not the school, responsible for his training and education. Therefore, you have the right to know what he learns and the responsibility to guard his spiritual development. In obedience to God, you must act when God shows you areas of spiritual danger or distortion.

☐ Pray as a family as well as alone. Pray for God's wisdom, timing, and direction—for His love and message to be communicated through you. Pray for openness and responsiveness in the people you will contact.

Keep in mind that most teachers try to do the best they can. Very few would consciously try to subvert your children. They merely apply the latest techniques presented to them at conventions or in-service sessions. These new ideas are like the tail of an elephant—they rarely reveal the character of the whole.

Convinced that their intentions are good, most teachers and principals will naturally become defensive if you confront them with anger or harshness. Pray, therefore, that God will enable you to see from their perspective and express genuine appreciation for their well-meaning efforts.

☐ Let the teacher know you care. Realize that a major reason why the school has assumed the responsibility for educating your child is its belief that most parents have abdicated theirs. Have you shown your interest by helping with classroom activities, joining in school activities, or perhaps driving for a field trip? Have you expressed your willingness to help the school provide a better education?

☐ Make an appointment with the teacher or school official you need to see.

☐ Let your outward appearance reflect God's peace and order. How you dress will probably affect their attitude toward you, as well as your own sense of confidence.

☐ Bring written notes of the facts that concern you. Be

prepared to suggest possible solutions to the problem.

□ Bring a tape recorder and *ASK PERMISSION* to use it. Recording the conference helps me review conversations, follow suggestions, and share information with my husband.

□ Be spiritually and emotionally ready to face resistance, defensiveness, and denial, but don't expect them. Cyndie Huntington, the founder of PASTIME (Parents and Schools Together Incorporating Meaningful Education) tells about one encounter with school officials:

> *When you reach this step, it is not unusual to be told, "Mrs. Jones, your child doesn't seem to have the problem, you do. Now what can we do to make YOU feel better?" or "We're the experts, let us raise your children."*
>
> *One PASTIME member was told by the principal to consider counseling for herself. Upon the recommendation of the school, she went to a secular counselor for two months of therapy.*
>
> *She stated that she counseled the counselor more than the counselor counseled her. It was then suggested by the school that she take the STEP (Steps to Effective Parenting) course. The school said that this would help her "interact" better with people and their children. So she signed up.*
>
> *At the second session, the instructor made the following statement: "No longer does the biblical principle of the wife being submissive to her husband and the children being submissive to both parents [apply] in society today. We are all equal. . . ."*
>
> *The mother asked the instructor what she should do if her ten-year-old did not want to clean her room. She was told that the room was the private property of the child and she should close the door if it bothered her; she had no right to enter without permission!*
>
> *She resigned herself to the fact that she did not have the problem, her child did not have the problem, the school system had the problem. She took her child out and put her in a private school.[1]*

□ Be familiar with the laws written to help you carry out your responsibilities. For example, if school officials refuse to show you special classroom projects, you can remind them of your legal rights as a parent.

–The Protection of Pupil Rights (Hatch) Amendment

states that "all instructional material, including teacher's manuals, films, tapes, or other supplementary instructional material which will be used in connection with any research or experimentation program or project shall be available for inspection by the parents or guardians of the children engaged in such programs or projects."[2]

–The "Equal Protection" Clause of the Fourteenth Amendment affirms that humanist or New Age educators have no more right to promote their religious views than do Christians. The constitutional interpretation that forbids prayer in school can work in our favor.

–Your state and school district may have other helpful laws. Check to see which ones would apply to your situation. Write to your U.S. senator and request federal and state level "Freedom of Information Acts."

David Schimmel and Lois Fischer, in their book *The Rights of Parents in the Education of Their Children,* summarize the scope of our legal rights:

> *The right to a free education, the right to be protected against harm, the right to inspect student records, the right to special education for students with special needs, the right to due process of law, the right to equal educational opportunity, the right of freedom from unreasonable search and seizure, the right to freedom of expression, and the right to freedom of religion and conscience.*[3]

Step Four: Enlist the Support of Other Christian Families

☐ Find other parents who share your concern. Your influence increases when parents stand together.

☐ Pray with other Christian parents. Always have prayer backing when you need to confront.

☐ Form small cell groups to discuss issues, compare notes, seek God's guidance, and plan strategy. Use tactics the secular community uses when it wants its voice heard. Go to the board meetings regularly and speak out! One salty but gracious voice can wield tremendous influence.

☐ Show your child that you understand the loneliness he

may feel in an anti-Christian classroom, and then remind him that he is not alone. Today God is training many children to follow His truth, no matter what it may cost. Pray together that God will provide a Christian friend who shares his commitment and can stand with him for what he believes. (This presupposes that he really knows and understands what he believes. So keep teaching God's truth.)

☐ If you have a less-than-desirable communication pattern with your child, pray that God will provide another adult confidant—someone for whom your child has respect and who also shares your views.

Equipping Your Elementary Child To Deal with Deception

☐ Know that you are the most important teacher in your child's life. So take time to share his struggles, read together, help with homework.

☐ Make sure your child has entered into a personal relationship with Jesus Christ. He must receive the Holy Spirit in order to understand biblical truth and discern the counterfeit.

☐ Continue to read and talk about God's Word.

☐ Explain the differences between God's truth and humanism—and between God's truths and New Age spirituality. Study the charts in chapter 1.

☐ Make a game of discovering examples of humanism and New Age spirituality. Review together the illustrations given at the beginning of chapter 1. Explain each conflict from God's point of view. As your child learns to see beliefs contrary to the truth, he will grow in discernment.

☐ Alert your child to some of the New Age buzzwords and phrases such as *centering, meditation, inner space, "imagine yourself flying," "feel yourself becoming,"* etc. While there is nothing wrong with the words themselves, New Agers have given them new meanings and may use them to invoke spiritual forces. You may want to scan the Glossary and explain other terms he encounters.

☐ Warn your child that meditation, guided imagery, ESP, and other spiritual or psychic techniques are not neutral exercises. They can bring him in contact with dangerous, supernatural forces—which God has told us to avoid. Discuss Deuteronomy 18:10-12 together: "Let no one be found among you ... who practices divination or sorcery, interprets omens, engages in witchcraft, or casts spells, or who is a medium or spiritist or who consults the dead. Anyone who does these things is detestable to the Lord."

☐ Explain the significance of God's armor. Practice putting it on together. Assure your child that this armor will keep him spiritually safe, no matter what spiritual forces surround him. Remind him that if coerced into being physically present during meditations, seances, or guided imagery, he need not be afraid or participate mentally. Instead, he should thank God for keeping him safe in the armor.

Equipping Your Teenage Child To Deal with Deception

☐ Be available. Your teenage child needs your participation in his life. He needs to see you as more dependable, caring, and understanding than his peers and teachers. Take time to enjoy as well as discipline, to play as well as pray.

☐ Listen! Give undivided attention! Be patient. Pray for understanding. Don't react with shock, dismay, or fear when your teenager shares what's happening in his world. Respond with gentle wisdom and compassionate love.

☐ Show appreciation. All too often I catch myself correcting and reminding more frequently than affirming and thanking. Ask God to show you good things to affirm daily.

☐ Provide information concerning humanism and New Age influences in the school. Suggest interesting books and articles he can read. Then plan times to discuss their relevance either one-to-one or as a family.

☐ If you question whether your teenager has a personal relationship with Christ, pray daily for openness to truth, contact with Christians, and an opportune moment when you or another Christian might lead him to Christ.

☐ Encourage him to read the Bible each day. He needs

to wear God's armor as much, if not more, than you—and that requires regular feeding on truth. Check your local Christian bookstore for a helpful Bible study for teenagers.

☐ Practice the habit of praying together. When you share your needs (with discretion) and ask for prayer, your teenager will find it easier to share his. When you show appreciation for God's answers and His wise, loving participation in your life (according to your teenager's capacity to listen), you are encouraging him to know, trust, and follow God.

☐ Be a friend as well as a parent. Show respect, trust (where earned), and genuine appreciation. By your attitude and words—make sure they match—you can give him a vision of what God wants to do in his life. Then walk with him—not ahead, pulling or behind, pushing—but at his side, gently encouraging, sharing, and supporting.

Children are a precious gift, an awesome responsibility and your greatest investment. Training them to follow God challenges your faith, demands your time, drains your energy, forces you to your knees, shows you God's sufficiency, and delights your heart. Hang in there—and "consider it pure joy" (James 1:2). "The One who calls you is faithful and He will do it" (1 Thessalonians 5:24).

SUGGESTED READING

Blumfield, Samuel L., *NEA—Trojan Horse in American Education*
Gabler, Mel and Norma, *What Are They Teaching Our Children?*

CHAPTER THREE
Schools and Values Clarification

Morals are sinking lower with every passing hour, and if they sink much lower . . . we will head straight into the arms of a dictatorship in this country, because America cannot survive without strong moral values. (Billy Graham)

Should schools teach values? They inevitably do. So the essential question is: Whose values?

Years ago, history books presented honorable heroes who modeled faith, courage, honesty, and integrity. Elementary readers introduced children to memorable characters who demonstrated genuine love, not a fleeting loving feeling, but the deep, laying-down-your-life kind of love that is so often ridiculed today.

A daring new curriculum has taken their place—texts that have been carefully combed for any trace of biblical bent. Literature free from "biased" words like *wife, husband,* or *marriage.* Books that emphasize reality and relevance by modeling adultery, dishonesty, and drug abuse.

Called *values clarification,* this "progressive" program challenges our children to defend or deny all the precious goals and guidelines of earlier days. It insists that the only true values are those a child chooses himself in response to his immediate needs, desires, and circumstances. It tells him, "Do your own thing!" The result is a growing social chaos among people who, like Israel during the time of the Judges, do what is "right in their own eyes."[1]

A mother from Kenosha, Wisconsin felt the painful effects of what her children were learning in school:

By the time my first two children had reached third grade, I realized something was wrong. The child I took to school in the morning was not the child I picked up after school in the afternoon. If this change had been a positive change, reflecting academic progress, I would have been delighted. However, the change I noticed was in their value system. They seemed to be desensitized to the morals I had been trying to instill in them as their mother, and I thought that I had failed. . . .

I failed because I had assumed that the schools my children were attending were like the schools I had attended.

I found instead that the thrust of schools had turned from education to indoctrination. I found the values I instilled in my children were not reinforced or respected by the schools, but were systematically challenged in the classroom.[2]

Spreading like cancer, this values transformation extends from the very core of our educational system to all its parts. In the name of progress, it promotes a self-centered kind of freedom from commitment, and self-control.

In transpersonal education, the learner is encouraged to be awake and autonomous, to question, to explore all the corners and crevices of conscious experience, to seek meaning, to test outer limits, to check out frontiers and depths of the self. (Marilyn Ferguson, *The Aquarian Conspiracy*)

Junior and senior high school students throughout Michigan were told to relax and "fantasize" in order to design a device for birth control "they would enjoy using." They were to discuss the criteria used for planning and the advantages of one design over another. Finally, they compared their design with existing contraceptives.[3]

What do students learn from this kind of exercise? The answer lies in the common goals of the humanist NEA, the New Age movement, and Planned Parenthood—three social forces that are surging forward together dead set on accomplishing their purpose.

BELIEFS AND GOALS OF

Humanist "NEA"	New Age	Planned Parenthood
"Traditional dogmatic or authoritarian religions that place God . . . above human needs and experience do a disservice to the human species."	"Intimacy is prized for its shared psychic intensity and transformative possibilities. . . . For many people, giving up the idea of exclusive relationships is the most difficult paradigm shift in their own transformation."[4]	Founder Margaret Sanger called sex the "radiant force" enabling mankind to attain "the great spiritual illumination which will transform the world, which will light the only path to an earthly paradise." How? "By expressing ourselves, by realizing ourselves more completely."[7]
". . . individuals should be permitted to express their sexual proclivities and pursue their lifestyles as they desire."	"When one begins the transformative process, death and birth are imminent: the death of custom as authority, the birth of the self. . . . "[5]	Faye Wattleton, current head and the 1986 Humanist of the Year, says, "Too many of us are focused upon stopping teenage sexual activity rather than stopping teenage pregnancy."[8]
"Happiness and the creative realization of human needs and desires . . . are continuous themes of humanism. We strive for the good life, here and now."	"A closed relationship, like a closed system in nature, loses energy."[6]	
(From *Humanist Manifesto II*)	(Marilyn Ferguson, *The Aquarian Conspiracy*)	

This hedonistic philosophy cannot bring fulfillment. Instead, it stirs insatiable cravings. Luring children into this sensuous, self-centered lifestyle is Satan's most effective way of turning them away from God. If they embrace sin, they cannot see God's glory (2 Corinthians 4:4).

Back to "Nature"

Humanism enflamed the intellectual community because it matched what they already believed. Likewise, Darwin's theory of evolution became an instant hit, because he put a plausible "scientific" framework around a myth that had already found acceptance—thus validating it. This explains why "creative" scientists could produce a full-bodied drawing of their mythological missing link from fractions of bones and get away with it. Though admittedly false, the familiar monkey-to-man line-up may remain in textbooks—as if true—until evolutionists find better "proof" for their popular beliefs. The probabilities of chance-evolution have been likened to that of a tornado sweeping through a scrap yard and accidentally forming a Boeing jet.

Far more than an attempt to explain origins, evolution has become a social philosophy—*the* way to view all of life. Evolutionists see man simply as a higher form of animal. Since we train animals to serve society, why not use psychological techniques like behavior modification in the classroom? Why not free children to exercise their *natural* instincts, satisfy their evolving animal nature, and thereby fulfill their human potential?

Humanist goals have not changed since Darwin's days. In fact, the educators who signed the Humanist Manifesto II in 1973 stressed a "natural" and evolutionary way of life.

In the area of sexuality, we believe that intolerant attitudes, often cultivated by orthodox religions and puritanical cultures, unduly repress sexual conduct. The right to birth control, abortion, and divorce should be recognized. . . . Moral education for children and adults is an important way of developing awareness and sexual maturity. (Humanist Manifesto II, 6)

Even before the signing of the revised manifesto, two innovative humanists, William Glasser and Sidney Simon, showed the way to implement it. Published in 1969, Dr. Glasser's book, *Schools Without Failure*, presented a "daring new program": The class, led by the teacher, would become a *counseling group*. Somehow, by airing uncomfortable circumstances and feelings each day, this encounter group was supposed to teach social responsibility and solve behavioral problems. Consider the effect of this suggestion by Dr. Glasser:

> *Children will often become very personal, talking about subjects that ordinarily are considered private. . . . The teacher should keep in mind that in class meetings, free discussion seems to be beneficial and that adult anxieties are often excessive. Nevertheless, a child who discusses drunken brawls at home might quietly be asked to talk about something that has more relationship to school.*
>
> *Changing the subject in this way is sometimes unwise, however, because it is just those drunken brawls at home that have the most relationship to his school progress.*[9]

Professor Sidney Simon went a step further. His book, *Values Clarification—A Handbook of Practical Strategies for Teachers and Students*, is packed with classroom exercises which filtered into textbooks and public schools. A popular strategy called *values voting* is "a simple and very rapid means by which every student in the class can make a public affirmation on a variety of values issues."[10]

The teacher simply asks a question. The students respond affirmatively by raising their hands. They give a negative reply by pointing their thumbs down. If undecided, they fold their arms. To pass, they do nothing. After the teacher has asked about ten questions, the class discusses the answers. Each child is forced to take a public stand— even if he passes. Imagine the effect of this kind of peer pressure on a child who feels insecure.

☐ The teacher asks, "How many of you . . .
    –think there are times when cheating is justified?
    –regularly attend religious services and enjoy it?

–think that women should stay home and be primarily wives and mothers?

–would like to have a secret lover?

–would choose to die and go to heaven, if it meant playing a harp all day?"[11]

Simon recommends this list for all ages. For secondary students, he adds questions such as: "How many of you think sex education instruction in the schools should include techniques for lovemaking, contraception?" and "How many of you think you will continue to practice religion, just like your parents?"[12]

You can see the rise of the New Age as a barometer of the disintegration of American culture. Dostoyevsky said anything is permissible if there is no God. But anything is also permissible if everything [or everyone] is God." (Robert J.L. Burrows, Spiritual Counterfeits Project, in "New Age Harmonies," *Time*, December 1987, 72)

Clarifying Values Clarification

Parents and teachers across the nation have agonized over the emotional damage caused by the psychological manipulations of Values Clarification. In response to their outcry, the Department of Education held hearings in seven locations across the country to implement the Protection of Pupil Rights (Hatch) Amendment.

Hundreds of parents testified at the hearings held in Seattle, Pittsburgh, Kansas City, Phoenix, Orlando, Concord (New Hampshire), and Washington, D.C. Phyllis Schlafly compiled excerpts from the official transcripts of the proceedings into an amazing book, *Child Abuse in the Classroom*. The reported violations fell into these categories:

☐ Bias against Christian values. A mother from Oregon, whose son became "very confused as to the rightness or wrongness of stealing," shared this testimony:

Young children are expected to fill in sentences such as, "the trouble with being honest is ____." They are asked, what would be the hardest thing for you to do: "steal, cheat, or lie?"

This question was discussed in the third grade: "How many of you ever wanted to beat up your parents?"[13]

☐ Bias toward humanist/New Age values. A first-grade lesson in "sex equity" shows the cruel pressure to conform.

The students each had two naked dolls, one male, the other female. They were asked to dress the dolls in work clothing to show that both genders could work at any job. . . . there were no dresses. All clothing was male-oriented. Then the teacher had the students sit in a circle while she pulled out objects from a sack, like a pancake turner or a tape measure. She asked, "Who uses this, mom or dad?"

If the students did not answer the way she had wanted, she would say, "Well, who else uses this?" Finally one little boy raised his hand and said, "I don't care. Men ought to be doctors and ladies nurses."

The teacher then asked how many of the students agreed with him. By the tone of her voice, they knew no one should raise a hand, so no one did. The little boy was so humiliated by the peer pressure and class manipulation . . . that he started to cry.[14]

Striving with religious zeal to convert children to "moral relativism" or "situational ethics," humanist educators argue that anything other than "value-free" teaching is religion. To them, only values that fit man's desires are valid. For if man is his own god, he has divine authority to choose his own rights and wrongs. Frequent name changes blocked the kind of "clarification" that would expose the mental manipulation. Programs might be called "values education," "self-awareness," "decision-making," "self-acceptance," or "interpersonal relation skills."

Values clarification is neutral, argues Simon, since every value is as valid as any other. To him, the only *wrong* position is one that believes in *absolute* values—and therefore opposes his belief that *all* values are relative.[15]

☐ Bias against traditional authorities such as parents and

the church. An eighth-grade sex education curriculum, titled "Are You Ready for Sex?" and used in Manistee, Michigan, asked questions such as: "Do you know why your parents and/or religion have taught that intercourse should wait until marriage? Do you accept these ideas? If so, would you be creating a lot of inner turmoil to go against your own beliefs?"[16]

Parents from New Jersey "could not find ... in any of the hypothetical situations, a single portrayal of parents in a positive manner. Parents were shown to be overreaching, nagging, unfair, overcritical of their children's friends." No wonder many children are confused about values, question their faith, and resist their parents.[17]

☐ Denial of the right to privacy. Values projects often require students to keep journals about their own and their parents' private activities. They are warned to tell no one.

Another popular technique makes home problems the focus of classroom discussion:

> *Earlier this year, my fifth grader came home from school telling me about a new classroom activity called Magic Circle. . . . He told me the children sit in a circle and tell each other positive and negative things about each other. The teacher is not a trained psychologist, and this type of group therapy can be harmful to a child if done improperly.*
>
> *I also resent the probing questions asked by the teacher in this setting:*
>
> *"How many of you have unemployed parents?"*
>
> *"How many of you have divorced parents?"*
>
> *"If any of you are abused sexually, I want you to tell me, because by law I have to report it."*

One mother summarized her feelings, "I consider this curriculum an invasion of family privacy, a subtle effort to erode all authority and undermine the traditional values that have made this nation great. . . ."[18]

☐ Practice of dangerous and destructive psychological techniques. The following attempts at Values Clarification, in a program called Preventive Guidance and Counseling, occurred in Lincoln County, Oregon. The parents learned

about the program *after* they determined to find out why
their children came home agitated on certain days.[19]

> *An eleven-year-old girl was placed in front of her counseling class
> to tell her feelings when she found her father dead. Upon disclosing
> this information, she was later hassled by classmates with teasing
> questions.*
>
> *A second child was forced, under threat of discipline to stand in
> front of the class and tell how it felt to have parents going through
> a divorce.*
>
> *A third child answering a questionnaire said, "Daddy spanks
> me, and sometimes pulls down my pants to spank me." Dad was
> then taken to the police station.[20]*

□ Concealment of strategies from parents. Many of the
ways schools gain private information about the home life
of its students are so subtle they escape notice. Often personal projects are hidden in curriculum that appear unre-
lated, such as physical education, English, or history. A
teacher in the Lansing, Michigan school district observed:

> *Students are all treated as in need or as having problems. Children
> are being pretested, then subjected to an affective [relating to feel-
> ings] values program as treatment for the disturbed child; then the
> child is post-tested to see what measurement of change has been
> produced by the affective values program.*
>
> *No parent has ever been notified or allowed to view the materi-
> als, nor have they ever consented to psychological diagnosis or
> treatment by an unlicensed psychologist or a psychiatrist. The
> children have even been promised that their parents won't be al-
> lowed to see their answers, "so be honest."[21]*

Are you wondering what happens to the data gathered
by tests and experiments? The above information on values
and behavior fed into computers and kept in student files
in an extensive data bank. Does this sound like "Big Brother" watching?

□ Peer pressure used for conforming children to group
standards—or to the values of the more popular students.
Concerning "sexual identity," Sidney Simon says, "The

schools must not be allowed to continue fostering the *immorality of morality*. An entirely different set of values must be nourished."[22] One of Simon's strategies, the *Values Continuum*, asks students to choose a position between two value-loaded alternatives:

How do you feel about premarital sex?

Virginal Virginia	*Mattress Millie*
wears white	*wears a*
gloves on	*mattress*
every date.	*strapped to her back.*

Sometimes students tend toward compulsive moderation in taking positions publicly. They place themselves right in the middle, thereby hoping to avoid conflict or the need to think critically. One thing the teacher can do if this occurs frequently is to simply eliminate the middle of the continuum. . . .

[Or] The continuum can be a real or imaginary line right down the center of the classroom. The students can actually place themselves on the line and negotiate with the people to their right and left to ascertain the correctness of their position. Students who are at the two opposite ends might profit from discussing their differences.[23]

□ Bias against self-sacrifice and toward self-gratification. Former Secretary of Education, William J. Bennett, and Edwin Delattre exposed the following strategy which was recommended for mealtime family discussion:

Your husband or wife is a very attractive person. Your best friend is very attracted to him or her. How would you want them to behave?

—Maintain a clandestine relationship so you wouldn't know about it.

—Be honest and accept the reality of the relationship.

—Proceed with a divorce.

Commenting on this exercise, Bennett and Delattre wrote, "Typically the spouse and the best friend are presented as having desires they will eventually satisfy anyway; the student is offered only choices that presuppose their relationship. All possibilities for self-restraint, fidelity, regard for others, or respect for mutual relationships and commitments are ignored."[24]

Apparently, educational psychology aims to "free" students to satisfy selfish cravings without ever feeling guilty. So they replace God's idea of service with the lie that man exists primarily to serve himself. In the end, what kinds of relationships will this attitude produce? What happens to a child's sense of self-worth when he and his peers learn to worship only themselves?

Apart from God, we have every reason to be discouraged. But God is greater than the social forces corrupting our nation. He has promised to "lead us in His triumph in Christ." In the light of His sufficiency, we can face unafraid the facts about our children's education.

"The student is led to believe that he or she has freedom to choose among meaningful alternatives, which on one level is partly true. But at the critical meta-ethical level, no choice or even mention of serious alternatives are presented. In fact, whenever other positions are mentioned, they are almost without exception presented in a highly biased language." (Richard A. Baer, Jr.)

Sex Education: Promotion or Prevention?

Adolescents need to know the physiology of sex and the dangers of promiscuous encounters. Their minds do not need to be steeped in envisioned delights and techniques of sexual intercourse.

Unfortunately, Planned Parenthood's philosophy pervades today's sex education: that children must be set free to indulge in sexual adventures without fear of pregnancy. Working together for social change, the NEA, Planned Parenthood, and SIECUS (The Sex Information and Education

Council of the United States) have prepared a titillating display of movies, textbooks, props, and promotional material. Most encourage rather than deter sexual activity.

Sexuality and Man, a collection of articles written and compiled by SIECUS board members, sports a yin-yang symbol on its cover. One of its authors, Lester Kirkendall, Ph.D., unveils the SIECUS philosophy: "The purpose of sex education is not . . . to control and suppress sex expression, as in the past, but to indicate the immense possibilities for human fulfillment that human sexuality offers. The individual must be given sufficient understanding to *incorporate sex most fruitfully* and most responsibly *into his present* and future life."

A much-used "value-free" text, *Changing Bodies, Changing Lives*, states: "People aren't born knowing how to be in sexual relationships, so you have to learn a lot with each partner."[25] Attempting to broaden this learning, it explains anal and oral sex and suggests that students may discover homosexual tendencies. "For some, that self-awareness and understanding is a natural and positive thing."[26] It tells how gay men make eye contact with strangers and hints that lesbians can meet through "shared political work in the woman's movement."[27] To students confronted by parents who don't want them to "be sexual at all until some distant time," it suggests that they may have to "tune out their [parents'] voice entirely."[28]

Like values clarification, sex education seems to be most "effective" in changing lifestyles when discussed openly. Therefore, the curriculum usually includes questions that stimulate the imagination and thus overcome modesty. Consider the discussion that could follow this question from the popular health guidance text, *Masculinity and Femininity:* "What are the advantages and disadvantages of using withdrawal to prevent conception?"[29]

While this text does mention abstinence as a possible means of birth control, it adds this comment: "Although agreeing that it works, many people do not consider abstinence to be a satisfactory choice."[30]

Obviously not. Studies show that today's teens generally believe they are entitled to enjoy sex. Anything goes, as long as they don't hurt or force anyone. Of course, "force" becomes very subjective when many (who have learned to affirm their greatness and follow their feelings) believe that a resisting partner really wants to be forced.

Assuming that children will indeed be sexually active, Planned Parenthood together with the Center for Population Options are planting school-based health clinics on campuses across the nation. These clinics provide birth control information, contraceptives, and abortion referrals for children as young as twelve. While a school cannot dispense an aspirin without a parent's consent, these clinics can provide abortion on demand without parental knowledge.

Ponder this chilling observation: In *The Aquarian Conspiracy*, Marilyn Ferguson quotes John Cuber, a sociologist at Ohio State University, who observed that the youth of 1969 had rejected the old sexual code:

> *It is a comfortable cliché among the middle-aged that the restive young, when faced with responsibilities, will settle into traditional viewpoints. That is not so for this generation. . . . As long as the sinner acknowledges his guilt, there is a chance that he may reform and repent. BUT THE KEY TO THIS GENERATION IS PRECISELY ITS FREEDOM FROM GUILT.*[31]

If people discredit truth and quench the conscience, how will they live? God points us to the answer:

> *There will be terrible times in the last days. People will be lovers of themselves, lovers of money, boastful, proud, abusive, disobedient to their parents, ungrateful, unholy, without love, unforgiving, slanderous, without self-control, brutal, not lovers of the good, treacherous, rash, conceited, lovers of pleasure rather than lovers of God. . . . In fact, everyone who wants to live a godly life in Christ Jesus will be persecuted, while evil men and impostors will go from bad to worse, deceiving and being deceived. But as for you, continue in what you have learned. (2 Timothy 3:1-4, 12-14)*

CHAPTER FOUR

What Can Parents Do About Values Clarification?

"These commandments that I give you today are to be upon your hearts. Impress them on your children. Talk about them when you sit at home and when you walk along the road, when you lie down and when you get up." (Deuteronomy 6:6-7)

Whether we like it or not, we know that our strongest messages flow through our lifestyles. Yet, even if we could live God's values perfectly, the model is incomplete without explanation. Our children need to know that our values come from God's Word, not from a personal preference. They need to hear and discuss God's ways until they can confidently explain them to others.

Children need to know WHY as well as WHAT. Hard-hitting questions will surely come from those who challenge their faith. Knowing the basis for their convictions, they will not waver when others declare that God's ways have become obsolete.

I remember Dad talking to me with tears in his eyes and saying, "I would give up my life—I would never vote for a political candidate who would kill one of those innocent little children." I remember his passion and I began to understand why. My passion today is a direct outgrowth of what he said to me back in those early days. (Dr. James Dobson, sharing his conviction concerning abortion)

Step One: Encourage Your Children To Love God

☐ Show your children how much you love God. Let them hear you pray, sing, thank Him, talk about Him, and make choices that honor Him.

☐ Show your own enthusiasm and commitment to knowing and hearing God speak to you through His Word.

☐ Read and discuss other books that tell about God.

☐ Share what God shows you. Tell how He helps you.

☐ Pray with your children each day for wisdom and strength. Ask God to live His life in and through you. Show that you rely on Him.

☐ Thank Him together for answers to prayers. Be specific.

☐ Practice living God's truth together, as you play games, eat meals, participate in sports, ride in the car, share your resources with others. Remember that all activities are opportunities to live for God and affirm your appreciation for what He values.

Step Two: Share God's Values with Your Child

☐ Ask God to show you how to communicate in natural age-appropriate ways. The simplest way is to discuss your own personal experiences from God's perspective during your ordinary encounters—when you "sit . . . walk [or drive] . . . lie down . . . and get up."

You may want to use the following topics and questions for meal or bedtime discussion or for special family evenings. Choose items appropriate to your children, adjusting the words to their age-level.

☐ Explore the meaning of *values*.

  –What does it mean to value something?

  –What do *you* value? Least? Most?

  –What determines your values?

  –What costs are you willing to pay for what you value? Rejection, teasing, not seeing certain movies?

☐ Discuss what God says about things He loves.

  –Honoring parents: Exodus 20:12

–Obeying parents: Ephesians 6:1
–Respecting authority: Romans 13:1
–Following God—our highest authority: Acts 5:29; John 10:4
–Love: 1 Corinthians 13:1-7
–Forgiving and caring for others: Luke 6:27-36
□ Discuss what God says about things He hates.
–Lying: Proverbs 12:22
–Stealing: Matthew 19:18
–Cheating: 1 Corinthians 6:8-9
–Greed: Luke 12:15
–Rudeness and swearing: Ephesians 5:3-5
□ Talk about what would happen if everyone followed this guideline: Do whatever feels right. How important are Judeo-Christian values to our society?

I have never asked my children's opinion about the truth of this value claim [that torture is wrong] and do not intend to do so, just as I never asked them their opinion about the law of gravity. . . . Rather, I teach them the truth of this value and expect them both to believe it and to base their action on it.
(Richard A. Baer, Jr.)[1]

Step Three: Train Your Children To Be "Ambassadors" for God

□ Tell your own experience of standing up for what you believe. Let your children feel *your* inner battle to choose God's way. Assure them that you understand their struggles—and that God's favor is worth far more than peer approval. No matter how we *feel*, we who belong to Him *are* His ambassadors (2 Corinthians 5:20).
□ Take time to read together stories about courageous Christians. Nobody outgrows the richness of family reading.
□ Practice sharing your convictions with each other. (1 Peter 3:15-17)

Step Four: Know What Values the School Teaches

America's obvious moral deterioration has fueled a growing demand for values education. Offered in an atmosphere that rejects biblical roots, values teaching will continue to grow out of the sandy foundation of moral relativism.

☐ Talk with your child about classroom activities.

☐ Scan texts, take-home projects, and fliers. Discuss movies and special classroom activities. Ask: Do they . . .

–Put down Christian values? Imply that honesty, loyalty, obedience, and sexual purity are outdated or negotiable? Recommend or model situational ethics?

–Present a negative view of parents? Suggest that parents are old-fashioned, too strict, or intrusive? Recommend that students ignore parents' advice and dismiss their guidelines?

–Require students to reveal or discuss private family matters? Ask embarrassing personal questions?

–Evidence the use of group counseling or psychological techniques? Tell your child to keep secret an assignment or project?

–Use peer pressure to conform children to popular standards and class consensus?

–Promote self-gratification rather than actions that produce patience, perseverance, and maturity?

☐ If any answer is yes, speak with the teacher or school officials. Follow the guidelines in chapter 2 of this book.

In January 1989 four schoolteachers sued the San Ramon, California school board and superintendent for forbidding the use of R-rated movies in the classroom. The two main thrusts of their complaint: (1) Their constitutional right to *free speech in the classroom*—even before a *captive audience* who must listen in order to pass tests; and (2) Prohibition of R-rated films is tantamount to teaching the religious view of a small minority of citizens.

☐ Examine the sex and/or AIDS education program. If it promotes sexual activity, join with other concerned parents, and suggest alternatives. Two excellent programs are: Sex Respect, which encourages teenagers to "say no," and Teen-Aid, which emphasizes "the deep meaning of sexuality in the context of the family." (Respect, Inc., Bradley, IL 60915; Teen-Aid, N. 1330 Calispel, Spokane, WA 99201)

Step Five: Seek Cooperation with Your Church

☐ Know what it offers your children. Find out what children's programs and youth groups are teaching. Ask:
–Do they teach the basic tenets of Christianity?
–Do they have a plan for teaching biblical values? The Ten Commandments is a simple and basic outline of God's values. The Sermon on the Mount (Matthew 5–7) shows the utter impossibility of keeping God's Laws by our own strength, and therefore reminds us to acknowledge our need and trust in His sufficiency.
☐ Encourage each other. Parents need to agree on standards, so that children realize that other families follow the same firm guidelines.
☐ Build a resource center. Share books, information, experiences, and concerns with other parents.

Step Six: Emphasize Values Through Political Involvement

Democracy and freedom are often taken for granted in America. You may want to help your children *value* these privileges by sharing your involvement in the political process. Many of our precious freedoms as parents are being challenged at all three political levels: local, state, and national. If we fail to speak up, these may vanish.

A Christian group, Committee on Moral Concerns, alerted the public to two bills submitted to the California legislature in 1988. Both died in the Assembly; if they had passed, they would have required (1) *mandatory sex education starting in first grade* and (2) *AIDS education,* with emphasis on homosexual acts, *starting in kindergarten.* Most of the policymakers in the school system are fighting for values opposite to ours. Therefore, Christians need to *stay alert* and *join together in Spirit-led resistance.* To receive current information about critical issues, subscribe to *Citizen,* a monthly magazine published by *Focus on the Family,* Pomona, CA 91799.

Projects for Adolescents

□ Talk together about the basic goals of sex education. In most places, these goals are not to prevent sexual activity but to release children from parental authority to a "new" sensual lifestyle. This fits humanist and New Age demands for a return to nature, for pleasure, and for enlightenment through ecstasy. It also closes doors to Christianity—most sexually active teens will shut out voices that question their chosen lifestyle.

□ Define and discuss words like . . .

–Love. What kinds? Based on what? (See 1 Corinthians 13:1-7; John 15:12-14; 1 John 4:7-12)

–Commitment. What is it? What are the costs?

–Respect. What makes you respect yourself? Others? Who are some of the people you respect? Why?

–Intimacy. What is it? How can teens be intimate without having sex? How can sex hinder intimacy?

–Chastity or virginity. What do they mean? Why are they good?

–Dating. Advantages of group dating? Disadvantages of group dating? How can you show love without sex?

–Abortion. Study these Scriptures for insight: Jeremiah 1:4-5; Psalm 127:3; 139:13-16; Luke 1:41-45.

□ Know what God says about your body in 1 Corinthians 3:16-17; 6:15-20.

□ Know what He says about sex outside marriage in Ephesians 5:3; 1 Thessalonians 4:3-5; and Genesis 39:7-9.

A study conducted in conservative Christian churches found that among teens who believe that Jesus is their personal Saviour and who also attend church weekly, forty percent have engaged in premarital sex.[2]

God made sex the most beautiful expression of intimacy and love possible between a man and a woman who are committed to each other. But outside marriage, it can cripple body and mind with excruciating emotional pain and lasting wounds. "When you have sex with someone, you are having sex with everyone they have had sex with for the last ten years, and everyone they and their partners have had sex with for the last ten years." (C. Everett Koop, former U.S. Surgeon General)

Steps to Victory

☐ See yourself as special and unique, belonging to God— created, planned, and guarded by Him.

☐ Be wise. Study God's guidelines. (Ephesians 5:15-18)

☐ Know your own weaknesses. Trust in God's strength. Decide to say NO to disobedience *before* you take the first step. Avoid compromising situations. (1 Timothy 4:7-8)

☐ Remind yourself . . .

–"His grace is sufficient in my weakness." 2 Corinthians 12:9-10

–"He lives in me." Galatians 2:20

–"I can do all things in Christ." Philippians 4:13

SUGGESTED READING

Phyllis Schlafly, *Child Abuse in the Classroom*

Jane Chastain, *I'd Speak Out On the Issues If I Only Knew What to Say*

Two monthly magazines, *Familywalk* and *Youthwalk*, offer relevant articles and daily discussion questions for families and teenagers. You can order them from *Focus on the Family*, Pomona, CA 91799.

CHAPTER FIVE
Schools and New Age Globalism

Who controls the youth, controls the future. (Adolf Hitler)

Under the guise of teaching world-mindedness, there is a growing element within the global education movement that wants children to adopt Eastern mystic/occult philosophy. Global education supposedly is to teach children that they are "citizens" of a global village. Mystic global educators go beyond political, economic, and technological subjects to delve into what they call "planetary consciousness." This "higher level" of global connectedness, they say, will bring about world peace and prosperity. (Eric Buehrer, National Association of Christian Educators)

A counterfeit hope surges through our society today: *We can do it!* We can re-create the earth and complete the evolutionary process. When we eliminate national barriers, we will be one. By joining consciousness around the world, we can become a superrace, the true global family of God.

The seeds of this utopian dream were sown by John Dewey. Nurtured by the warm friendship between humanist NEA and UNESCO, one-worldism sank its roots deep into every level of public education. Dr. Robert Muller, Under-Secretary of the United Nation's Economic and Social Council, unmasks the movement's spiritual nature in his book on global education, *New Genesis: Shaping a Global Spirituality:*

On a universal scale, humankind is seeking no less than its reunion with the "divine," its transcendence into ever higher forms

58

of life. Hindus call our earth Brahma, or God, for they rightly see
no difference between our earth and the divine. This ancient sim-
ple truth is slowly dawning again upon humanity . . . as we are
about to enter our cosmic age and to become what we were always
meant to be: the planet of God.[1]

To "evolving" New Agers, the dream of global oneness
justifies any questionable means. It is not surprising then to
find classrooms teaching steps toward fulfilling this lofty
vision. The formula that substitutes counterfeit values for
God's wisdom can also change the world: crush the old;
then out of the ashes will rise a new earth—a world free
from guilt, fear, oppression, and poverty. The time is ripe to
buy the lie.

"Beginning with the school year of 1982–83, global citizenship was
being taught to the kids instead of American citizenship. This was
mandated through the National Council of Social Studies teachers." (Dr. William M. Bowen, Jr.)[2]

This transformation is accelerating as millions around
the globe await the New Age world of harmony, love, and
oneness—a world of evolved god-men all following the
wisdom of Self.

The New American History

The New Age balloon has two major flaws. It ignores the
selfish nature of man and the sovereign plan of God. Yes,
the Bible tells us that a one-world government will rise to
power waving the banner of peace. But it will unleash un-
imaginable cruelty and oppression. Like ancient Babylon, it
will demonstrate both the captivating power of Satan and
the base depravity of man separated from God.

Those who buy the lie that the end justifies the means
usually discover that the means foretells the end. We can

catch a glimpse of a future New Age world by looking at the ways its people pursue their goals. If they deceive during the pursuit, they will deceive in the end.

We know that totalitarian governments distort historical facts in order to control their people—but America would never stoop to that, would it? In their book, *What Are They Teaching Our Children?* Mel and Norma Gabler present some chilling facts:

☐ *Who deserves more attention in an American history text: George Washington or Marilyn Monroe? One fifth-grade text devoted seven pages to Miss Monroe, while mentioning George Washington only eight times.*

☐ *Name the nation you think is being discussed in this passage from another fifth-grade text: "No nation on earth is guilty of practices more shocking and bloody than is ____ at this very hour. Go where you may and search where you will. Roam through all the kingdoms of the Old World. Travel through South America. Search out every wrong. When you have found the last, compare your facts with the everyday practices of this nation. Then you will agree with me that, for revolting barbarity and shameless hypocrisy, ____ has no rival." Give up? The country so honored is the United States.*

☐ *Name six major culture areas of the world. If you included the United States and Western Europe in your list, you're wrong— at least according to a world history text which selects: the Soviet Union, Latin America, China, India, Africa, and the Middle East.*

☐ *Fill in the blank. "[In China] ____ turns the people toward a future of unlimited promise, an escalator to the stars." The missing word is Marxism.*

☐ *Patrick Henry sounded the watchword of American independence: "Give me liberty or give me death!" Is this line worth memorizing by children? According to a study made by* This Week *magazine, only* two *of* forty-five *history texts include his statement.*[3]

While other nations whitewash their past, our country grants global-minded educators the freedom to reduce our nation's image to that of a greedy, aggressive tyrant. They warned us, but we didn't believe it could happen. In their

Manifesto II, humanists told us that they "deplore the division of humankind on nationalistic grounds" and aim to "transcend the limits of national sovereignty." They are determined to build "a world community"—with the help of our children. A textbook for teachers said:

> *Allegiance to a nation is the biggest stumbling block to the creation of international government. National boundaries and the concept of sovereignty must be abolished. The quickest way to do this is to condition the young to another and a broader alliance. Opinion favorable to international government will be developed in the social studies in the elementary school.*[4]

"The public schools will be the propaganda outlet for those advocating the "One World" doctrine. The schools are being inundated with propaganda promoting the concept of INTERdependence—which emphasizes 'global perspectives' and 'global citizenship.'" (Marlin Maddoux, host of *Point of View*)

Peace Education

The depreciation of America and the proclamation of the globalist view of peace are programming children to accept four New Age goals:

□ A New World Order, which implies a one-world government.

□ A new world religion. The New Age medley (syncretism) of humanism, Hinduism, and every other religion—except genuine Christianity—fits the bill perfectly.

□ A new economic system to redistribute the world's wealth—especially America's.

□ A spiritually evolved global citizenry ruled by the most advanced and most aware.

To steer students into the one-world camp, globalists use a strategy called "Management by Crisis." Their prod is fear, and the programming may begin as early as kindergarten. This "peace curriculum" first immerses the children in genuine concerns blown to crisis proportion—such as the horrors of nuclear war and ecological disaster—then uses predetermined reactions for political purposes.

To avoid confrontation with "right-wing Christian groups," a memorandum from the Seattle Public Schools dated April 19, 1985 recommends using terms other than "Global Education." A "temporary, safe term is multi-cultural/international curriculum development."[5]

[The political movement behind peace studies] has urged that our schools institute "infusion workshops" in which teachers set aside days "to grow in enthusiasm for justice and peace education." This is not education; this is indoctrination. (William Bennett, former U.S. Secretary of Education)

With the excuse that children's fear had to be brought out in the open, globalist educators found ways to produce the needed fear. Children watched films showing mutilated victims from the Hiroshima and Nagasaki bombings.[6] They were told to discuss the long-term effects on "those who are not immediately killed by the explosion." They pondered the ongoing pain of radiation sickness. They studied pictures drawn by Hiroshima survivors. They played games to stir thoughts about their own death. They imagined the devastation from far larger nuclear explosions in their own state, county, and neighborhood. And they became afraid.

They heard strange accounts about America's aggressive, uncooperative policies. They learned to sympathize with Russia's struggles with unfriendly neighbors. They played games to prove American wealth and greed in the face of a starving world community.

They became angry and felt ashamed. At that point a trained teacher could direct their fear, anger, and national guilt into desirable action—make scrapbooks on peace, tell adults about disarmament, share at community forums, write letters to their senators—and to the President.[7]

If global education taught facts rather than feeling, discernment rather than sympathy, and reality rather than propaganda, we would applaud it. But it doesn't. It teaches children to scorn America, favor Russia, and despise our national leadership. It leads them to sincerely but arrogantly believe that their naive solutions are better than those based on wise consideration of historical data, the oppression of dictatorships, and the horrendous injustices of Communism.

Deploring this political subversion in our schools, William Bennett, then United States Secretary of Education, remarked:

> *Nor is it proper to use American classrooms for "creating a grassroots network of educator activists" as Educators for Social Responsibility . . . described its goal. . . .*
> *Wishes will not replace the fact that American citizens share almost nothing of their political life with the subjects of a totalitarian government. . . . All men are created equal; but all political and social systems are not.[8]*

The Hundredth Monkey

To inspire children with a sense of power to change their world, many peace programs use the following fable as a guiding principle. The fact that it evolved from real events makes the fiction credible.

The story began with a group of Japanese scientists who studied macaque monkeys on the island of Koshima in 1952. When they left some yams—a new treat—on the beach, a young female monkey improved the taste by washing off the sand in nearby water. First the younger monkeys imitated her actions, soon the others followed.

Here factual reporting gives way to New Age myth-making. In the fictional story used by several peace programs, Imo, a young female, taught the trick to her mother. Then her smart little playmates who copied her taught the trick to their mothers. The next point is significant: "Only the adults who imitated their children learned this social im-

provement. Other adults kept eating the dirty sweet pota-
toes." At this point the myth soars into the realm of magic.

> *In the autumn of 1958, a certain number of Koshima monkeys*
> *were washing sweet potatoes—the exact number isn't known. Let*
> *us suppose that when the sun rose one morning there were ninety-*
> *nine monkeys on Koshima Island who had learned to wash their*
> *sweet potatoes. Let us further suppose that later that morning, the*
> *hundredth monkey learned to wash potatoes. THEN IT*
> *HAPPENED!*
>
> *By that evening almost everyone in the tribe was washing sweet*
> *potatoes before eating them. The added energy of this hundredth*
> *monkey somehow created an ideological breakthrough!*
>
> *But notice. The most surprising thing observed by these scien-*
> *tists was that the habit of washing sweet potatoes spontaneously*
> *jumped over the sea—colonies of monkeys on other islands and the*
> *mainland troop of monkeys at Takasakiyama began washing their*
> *sweet potatoes!*
>
> *Thus, when a certain critical number achieves an awareness,*
> *this new awareness may be communicated from mind to mind.*
> *Although the exact number may vary, the Hundredth Monkey Phe-*
> *nomenon means that when only a limited number of people know*
> *of a new way, it may remain the consciousness property of these*
> *people. But there is a point at which if only one more person tunes*
> *in to a new awareness, a field is strengthened so that this aware-*
> *ness reaches almost everyone! . . . Your awareness is needed in*
> *saving the world from nuclear war. You may be the "Hundredth*
> *Monkey."* [9]

Like Darwin's theory of physical evolution, the hundredth monkey fantasy has been grasped as "scientific"
basis for the New Age dream, both inside and outside the
field of education. No wonder! It presents the ultimate in
spiritual evolution. And in the subjective atmosphere of the
New Age, you don't question a revelation. You just believe!

The tale of the hundredth monkey became a popular
myth—powerful enough to shape New Age creed. People
believed it—and acted on it. For example, a few years ago,
Randolph Price, who heads the networking Planetary Commission, called for a special day of global meditation.

*We see that the world consciousness is quickly moving toward
critical mass. . . . Doing whatever is necessary to change our individual consciousness, we will begin to break up some of the dark
pockets of negative energy in the race mind. Through our collective
efforts on December 31, 1986, we can literally turn on the Light of
the World, dissolve the darkness, and begin the New Age of spirituality on Planet Earth.*[10]

A New World Religion

To inspire a consciousness explosion, many New Age leaders are determined to win a critical mass of minds. Children would be the prime target of the missionary efforts,
and schools their greatest battlefield.

William Bennett exposes this ominous blend of public
school curriculum, New Age spirituality, and cosmic
dreams:

*Another legacy from the Age of Aquarius that has been enshrined
in too many of our social studies curricula is a disturbing
antirational bias. Curriculum guides for . . . global education are
shot through with calls for "raised consciousness," for students
and teachers to view themselves "as passengers on a small cosmic
spaceship," for classroom activities involving "intuiting," "imag-
ing," or "visioning" a "preferred future."*

*Two proponents of such curricula have offered a candid cau-
tion: "These exercises may seem dangerous to your logical thought
patterns. For best results, suspend your judging skills and prepare
to accept ideas that seem silly and/or impractical." Well, if we're
going to give up critical judgment, we'd better give up the game of
education altogether.*[11]

While "raised consciousness" and "visioning" sound too
mystical for admission into many schools, a new form of
religious education does not. Teaching about the major
world religions such as Buddhism, Hinduism, Islam, and
Christianity, the curricula emphasize the universal "truths"
and historical values of each. That sounds fair and innocuous, until we remember that New Age globalism calls for a

one-world religion—a persuasive union of all supposed paths to eternal life. Since biblical Christianity doesn't fit the formula, some of these courses have—in the hands of "progressive" teachers—become a platform for criticizing Christian exclusiveness and promoting Eastern meditation.

Speaking to many of the world's religious and political leaders in 1988, Robert Runcie, the Archbishop of Canterbury, articulated this New Age formula for spiritual oneness in a global community. Notice the apologetic and compromising version of "Christianity":

> *Behind [this resurgence of religions] lies a widespread pessimism about the future of humankind, and unsatisfied longing for alternative paths to salvation. . . .*
>
> *All the centuries that the Spirit of God had been working in Christians, He must also have been working in Hindus, Buddhists, Muslims, and all the others. . . . This will mean that some claims about the exclusiveness of the Church will have to be renounced. . . .* [12]

In April of 1988, representatives of Christianity, Buddhism, Hinduism, Islam, and Judaism met with political leaders from over forty nations to "solve" the world's problems. This Global Conference of Spiritual and Parliamentary Leaders on Human Survival was sponsored by the Temple of Understanding. Founded with the support of such dignitaries as the Dalai Lama, Indian Prime Minister Nehru, Eleanor Roosevelt, Popes John XXIII and Paul VI, the Temple has become a "hotbed of international dialogue and outright promotion of eastern mysticism." Among its recent guest speakers are New Age advocates like Donald Keys, David Spangler, and Benjamin Creme who continues to herald the coming of Lord Maitreya, "The Christ." [13]

For false Christs and false prophets will appear and perform great signs and miracles to deceive even the elect—if that were possible. (Matthew 24:24)

The Sin of Separateness

Because unity is essential for creating the critical mass, many New Age leaders join in condemning the hindering influence of the church. Their objection? Its "negative energy" blocks the envisioned evolutionary breakthrough. As you have seen, this belief has filtered into the classroom.

Thus, anyone who follows God becomes guilty of the only sins in the New Age: unbelief and separateness. Christians who refuse to share the global vision and join the evolutionary march will reap persecution. "In fact, everyone who wants to live a godly life in Christ Jesus will be persecuted" (2 Timothy 3:12). For Satan, the counterfeit angel of light, hates all who shine the true light of Christ into the world.

God is not surprised at this diabolical deception. Long ago, He warned us that the Antichrist would one day rule the world and persecute Christians:

> *He was given power to make war against the saints and to conquer them. And he was given authority over every tribe, people, language, and nation.*
>
> *All inhabitants of the earth will worship the beast—all whose names have not been written in the Book of Life belonging to the Lamb that was slain from the creation of the world. (Revelation 13:7-8)*

Meanwhile, God calls us to remain separate. As His holy people, we cannot join the forces of the Antichrist:

> *Do not be yoked together with unbelievers. For what do righteousness and wickedness have in common? Or what fellowship can light have with darkness? . . . What agreement is there between the temple of God and idols?*
>
> *For we are the temple of the living God. As God has said, "I will live with them and walk among them, and I will be their God, and they will be My people. Therefore come out from them and be separate." (2 Corinthians 6:14-17)*

Since our children belong to God, He takes care of them.

If they have to share in some of the persecution, He will be with them to protect, shield, and to give spiritual compensations that far exceed the suffering. Let Him encourage your family with this promise:

> *Be strong and courageous. Do not be afraid or terrified because of them, for the Lord your God goes with you; He will never leave you nor forsake you. The Lord Himself goes before you and will be with you. . . . Do not be afraid; do not be discouraged. (Deuteronomy 31:6, 8)*

Death Education

The most bizarre part of global education is that in which children are encouraged to explore their feelings about death. To make sure they have feelings to explore, students visit cemeteries and funeral homes, try out coffins, watch an embalming, plan their own funerals, write their own obituaries, design their own gravestones, and practice writing suicide notes.[14]

In line with Simon's values clarification, these programs emphasize that suicide is a matter of personal preference and choice. With that bit of encouragement, students discuss reasons for dying and fantasize about the means of ending their own lives.

Are American public schools teaching children to hate life and love death? The answer is a resounding yes. How is this done? Through lessons in values clarification which teach hatred of life, and lessons in death education which teach love of death. (Samuel Blumenfeld, author of *NEA: Trojan Horse in American Education*)

Simulation games such as Lifeboat and Radiation Shelter force children to make life-and-death decisions based on what is "relevant" and "the greatest good for the greatest number."[15] Students have to answer questions such as: Who should be thrown overboard to the sharks in order to save the rest: a singer, a doctor, a clergyman? Which family member must die in the nuclear holocaust (or in a cave or in a boat accident): mother, father, brother, sister, or self ... ?[16] Imagine the resultant confusion, nightmares, fears, and guilt in insecure children.

These exercises may be part of any class. For example, an eighth-grade English textbook used in Hingham, Massachusetts told students to write suicide notes. It gave a "relevant" example which included this suggestion: "I can't communicate with my parents. [They] don't understand me. . . . "[17]

The University of Kentucky developed a "simulation mind game" in which the teacher guides the pupils through "a sort of seance" in a dim candlelit room. The students are told, "You will experience death and at that moment you will see yourself rise to the ceiling of this room . . . [and be] content in your new state."[18]

Gregg L. Cunningham was an official in the Education Department's regional office in Denver until he wrote a candid report exposing the globalist program of the Center for Teaching International Relations. Ponder his observation:

> *For unsurpassed morbidity . . . students can consider a lament that our culture does not "encourage visits" from "the spirits of the dead" (described as an "open and joyous" experience in contrast with American "uncomfortable" attitudes toward the dead).[19] They are then taught to "create their own altar honoring the dead" (in a manner reminiscent of ancestor worship).[20]*

Who promotes these courses that encourage depression and suicide? Ecologists who want to reduce the world's population to save resources? Proponents of eugenics who, like Hitler and Margaret Sanger, envision a superrace rid of its weaker or less-conforming members? Militant social reformers who want to desensitize youth to organized euthanasia and other forms of social killing? New Age missionaries who want to present death as a way to escape the present for a better tomorrow through reincarnation. Or New Age visionaries preparing our youth for the prophesied purge of all who commit the sin of separateness—who hinder the plan by not joining the march toward the new global society?

Most likely, all of the above. God says, "All who hate Me love death." The counterfeit army that hates God's people embraces death education and other deadly philosophies.

God's Encouragement

Our children are not immune to the world's messages. They hear the same tempting voices, the same "positive affirmations" that others hear and follow. Concerned about their spiritual safety, our Shepherd reminds them: "Don't let the world around you squeeze you into its own mold, but let God remold your minds from within, so that you may prove in practice that the plan of God for you is good" (Romans 12:2-3, PH).

Unless we help our children build a mental framework and filter based on biblical truth, the world's philosophies will squeeze them into its mold. Therefore it is essential that they see God as the only ultimate source of wisdom, power, and triumph.

> *The Lord is my rock, my fortress and my deliverer;*
> *my God is my rock, in whom I take refuge.*
> *He is my shield and the horn of my salvation,*
> *my stronghold.*
> *I call to the Lord, who is worthy of praise,*
> *and I am saved from my enemies. (Psalm 18:2-3)*

CHAPTER SIX

What Can Parents Do About New Age Globalism?

The best global education for American students is the truth—the truth about ourselves, our political culture, and our intellectual legacy. And the truth about the world, in all its friendly and hostile aspects, for all its good and all its evil. (William Bennett)

We can read some of God's most practical truths in the Old Testament. He told His precious people that success would come from knowing, loving, trusting, and following Him. On the other hand, if they were to spurn His counsel, they would lose His protection and become slaves of foreigners.

His people forgot. Growing strong and comfortable in the rich land God had given them, they became complacent and ignored His warnings. The result? They lost everything—possessions, lives, the Promised Land, and the comfort of God's presence. Longing to save us from similar consequences, God reminds us through Paul, "These things occurred as examples, to keep us from setting our hearts on evil things as they did" (1 Corinthians 10:6).

When Israel followed God's guidelines, it enjoyed His protection, peace, and prosperity. This same principle applies in the spiritual Kingdom where we, God's people, live with our King. In either homeland, the key to success lies in His ancient instructions to Israel:

Love the Lord your God with all your heart and with all your soul and with all your strength. These commandments that I give you today are to be upon your hearts. Impress them on your children. (Deuteronomy 6:5-7)

If you pay attention to these laws and are careful to follow them, then the Lord your God will keep His covenant of love with you. . . . You will be blessed more than any other people. (7:12, 14)

When you have eaten and are satisfied, praise the Lord your God for the good land He has given you. Be careful that you do not forget the Lord your God, failing to observe His commands. . . . Otherwise, when you eat and are satisfied, when you build fine houses and settle down . . . then your heart will become proud and you will forget the Lord. (8:10-14)

America today follows a dangerous path. In her pursuit of lesser gods, our nation is risking the loss of freedom. But if we will turn to God, He will protect our families and may extend the time of peace in this land.

If My people, who are called by My name, will humble themselves and pray and seek My face and turn from their wicked ways, then will I hear from heaven and will forgive their sin and will heal their land. (2 Chronicles 7:14)

Step One: Knowing and Loving God

☐ Continue a family Bible reading program appropriate to your child's age. Look at God together, see Him as He really is—not as the world distorts Him.

☐ Help your child see his identity from God's perspective. We are Americans, but more importantly, we are citizens of God's kingdom. He is our only hope for genuine and lasting peace, no matter what happens around us (Philippians 3:20; 1 John 3:1-3; Ephesians 1:1-10).

☐ Help your child to appreciate God's hand in building our country. Teach him about . . .

–the historical foundation for American democracy. Point out that many people fled to America because they had experienced religious persecution. Seeking God's guidance, they carefully established governmental checks and balances in order to preserve their precious new freedom.

–the development of our country. Peter Marshall, Jr. wrote an excellent book, *The Light and the Glory,* which shows God's loving hand in our nation's growth.

–the influence of faithful Christian leaders who trusted God, followed His ways, and built His truths into the foundations and fabric of this nation.

☐ Train your child to understand . . .

–the worth of our freedom to worship and follow God. Tell about faithful Americans who have laid down their lives for freedoms which some of today's citizens discredit, deny, or take for granted.

–the worth of our God-given privilege to influence public policies on all levels of government. America's willingness to hear all kinds of ideas—even revolutionary ones—proves its tolerance and freedom. However, apart from God, this freedom can destroy our nation.

America is great because America is good, and if America ever ceases to be good, America will cease to be great. (Alexis De Tocqueville)

Step Two: Know God's Instructions and Warnings

☐ As a family, read Deuteronomy 6–8. With younger children, you may want to use the Living Bible and preselect the most appropriate sections. Study a portion each day. Write and discuss *what He tells you to do* and *what He promises to do for you.* Agree to help each other to follow His guidelines and receive His promises.

☐ Show your child that while global understanding and cooperation is essential, the New Age quest for a global community is based on the evolutionary presumption that man—not God—controls and can save the world.

You may want to read together *Lord of the Flies* by William Golding (a frequent sixth-grade assignment). It illustrates the nature of man, the power struggle between good and evil, and the cruel dominance of the most devious aggressor.

□ Summarize the differences between American democracy and the aggressive, authoritarian, and anti-Christian policies of Communist governments and military dictatorships.

□ Show how commitment to truth grows from biblical values. While loving the world's people, we cannot trust rulers who oppose God and reject His values.

One of the most misunderstood and misquoted Scriptures in the Bible is Luke 6:37: "Do not judge, and you will not be judged." God is not telling us to close our eyes to evil and tolerate beliefs and behavior that deny Him. Rather He reminds us to "judge with the right judgment."

Hinduism teaches New Agers to tune out unpleasant realities. But no amount of creative visualization or joint wishful thinking will create a perfect world. The fact is that mankind apart from God still suffers from a deadly urge to

---

Global Education Associates (GEA) designed an "Earth pledge," which begins *"I pledge allegiance to the Earth."* GEA is a growing network of individuals in more than fifty countries. It has declared that "the human community is straining to break through the straitjacket of obsolete national paradigms to a viable world community" and it supports world order with a [pantheistic] "whole-earth spirituality." (D.L. Cuddy, a former consultant in the U.S. Department of Education)[1]

---

conquer and control. For instance, the welcome displays of Russian friendliness (1987–1989) demonstrate changed tactics but not necessarily transformed goals. Warning us to guard against deception, Peter Lalonde summarizes a Pentagon report entitled "Terrorists Group Profiles," which you can order from the U.S. Government Printing Office:

Thus, while with one hand the Soviets have been recently holding out promises to cut defense spending and reduce troop strength in

Europe, with the other they have continued relentlessly to fund, train, and advise terrorists eager to brutalize and intimidate political opponents into accepting communism.[2]

Whether or not contemporary Communism, masked by peace-and-freedom idealism, plays a major role in establishing the New World Order, it does illustrate the process of deception. Read the following description from *Beyond the Wall* by Hank Paulson, a missionary to Eastern Europe. Compare it to humanist/New Age demands for "freedom" from traditional authority, beliefs, and values.

The avowed purpose of communism is to impose its definition of Utopia upon the whole world. This is called "setting the masses free." Communism teaches young people to blame society or their parents instead of themselves for the restrictions they experience. Freed of responsibility for the consequences of their own behavior, people begin to condemn the social structures around them.[3]

Step Three: Guard Against Influences That Oppose God

Scan all textbooks, fliers, extracurricular information, school newsletters. Keep in mind that globalism may be disguised under other titles. Ask . . .

☐ Do they indicate that New Age global propaganda has filtered into traditional classes such as English and science?

My son David described a movie he saw in his eighth-grade science class: "A boy grew up in a family that believed in loyalty to the country. He enlisted in the army, went to war, but came home a quadriplegic. A kind nurse wanted to help him end his miserable existence, but the doctor refused to let him die." Notice who the villains are in the story.

☐ Do they bait children with emotional and extreme suggestions concerning nuclear disaster, global death from atomic warfare, and the collapse of the ecosystem?

Why this emphasis on destruction? Because it prepares this growing generation to accept peace at any cost.

A take-home flier from our neighborhood elementary school invited parents and educators to attend a conference on "Our Children's Future . . . Creating a New Possibility." Behind this "positive" invitation looms a large New Age organization called "Creative Initiative" or "Beyond War." Started by a Stanford University professor in the '60s, it bases its teachings on Teillard de Chardin's *The Phenomenon of Man*—a persuasive theory of man's spiritual evolution toward a utopic "Noosphere" of peace and oneness.

When fear intensifies, the promise of global peace may seem as appealing as the bowl of soup for which Esau sold his birthright to Jacob. We all hate war and long for peace—but not at the cost of our freedom!

Jesus said, "When you hear of wars and rumors of wars, do not be alarmed. Such things must happen, but the end is still to come. Nation will rise against nation. . . . There will be earthquakes in various places, and famines. These are the beginning of birth pains" (Mark 13:7-8).

☐ Do they suggest that meditative exercises may be used in the classroom to encourage children to visualize a New Age world community? Remember that such consciousness-raising exercises are usually hidden behind innocuous names or included in regular classroom subjects.

☐ Do they sensationalize or exaggerate the problems and dangers of global pollution? Do they use this information to direct children toward planned, biased political action?

☐ Do they emphasize suicide? Do they condone suicide as a viable solution to pollution or overpopulation?

☐ Do they promote any form of eugenics or euthanasia to solve the problems of overpopulation? Does your child participate in survival games that force him to choose who should live and die in hypothetical situations?

Step Four: Act on What God Has Shown You

☐ Pray alone and as a family for wisdom and for the capacity to love the deceived while abhorring the deception.

☐ If deceptive teaching compels you to act, it is best to join with other parents. You *can* make a difference alone, but your influence grows with numbers.

The National Association of Christian Educators—Citizens for Excellence in Education (NACE-CEE) helps parents work together for godly values and a good education. You may want to form a chapter in your school district. If so, write or call for information, tapes, and manuals at P.O. Box 3200, Costa Mesa, CA 92628, (714) 546-5931.

☐ When necessary, discuss problems and possible solutions with teachers or school officials.

☐ Learn about U.S.–Soviet Education Agreements to work together in developing a global curriculum. Robert Muller said in March 1985, "A world core curriculum might seem utopian today. By the end of the year 2000 it will be a down-to-earth, daily reality in all the schools in the world." Don't let it happen! Write your congressman for information about the U.S.–Soviet Exchange Initiative.

☐ **Share your concerns with officials.** Just as globalist programs point children to political action, so can we.

Write your Senators at the Senate Office Building, Washington, D.C. 20510.

Write your Congressman at the House Office Building, Washington, D.C. 20515

☐ Discuss and memorize this promise. Count on it! Live it! "Thanks be to God! He gives us the victory through our Lord Jesus Christ. Therefore, my dear brothers, stand firm. Let nothing move you. Always give yourself fully to the work of the Lord, because you know that your labor in the Lord is not in vain" (1 Corinthians 15:57-58).

SUGGESTED READING

Beyond the Wall by Hank Paulson
When the World Will Be One by Tal Brooke
Winterflight by Joseph Bayly
The Children's Story by James Clavell

PART TWO

MEDIA

CHAPTER SEVEN
Movies and Persuasion
by Identification

Moving images are irresistible. They attract the eye, engage the attention, and stir the mind. Therefore, the "visual media"—movies and television—are powerful tools of communication. (Spiritual Counterfeits Project)

In 1977, a youth pastor took our thirteen-year-old son Todd to see *Grease*. You probably remember it—a movie written for the '70s to highlight the '50s. The next evening my husband and I went to see it. I was shocked to think that a trusted church leader had brought junior high boys to a movie that modeled promiscuity and applauded a heroine who turned from morality to permissiveness.

"Don't worry," said the youth leader a few days later. "I taught them how to evaluate the movie. It can't hurt them."

Can't it? What about the exposure to pictures that are stored in the brain? What about the memories of a process that makes morality seem narrow-minded, cold, and judgmental, and makes evil seem kind and good? What about the manipulation that occurs when youngsters identify with the hero and participate emotionally with the good and bad choices of the characters?

Sensual pictures, mystical visions, and tempting suggestions don't immunize their viewers against wrongs. Rather, they desensitize the conscience and stir a craving for more. Stored in the brain, the enticing stimuli continue to influence the mind whether we recognize it or not.

Discussing the pictures afterward can't erase those stored images. Glimpses of immoral activities, identifica-

The chroniclers and even the advertisers have noticed a growing and apparently *insatiable popular appetite for mystery and self-transcendence.* In early 1987 alone, an exponential growth has generated a fresh momentum, an acceleration in the rate of acceleration. (Marilyn Ferguson in *The Aquarian Conspiracy*)

tion with characters who oppose God, and memories of the apparent triumph of evil . . . these become building blocks in a child's value system.

When I saw *Grease,* I too felt the pull of the world's value system. First I silently cheered the sweet, innocent girl who stood firm in what she believed. But the growing tension between the hero's unsatisfied sexual desires and the heroine's moral stand kindled a desire for a resolution. In the end, the heroine donned black, sexy, skintight wrappings—the symbol of her choice to discard the values that "deprived" the one she loved. While disgusted with her foolish decision and destructive modeling, I found myself sharing the audience's relief for what seemed to be the only *comfortable* solution to the problem.

Did my values change? No. But for a moment I was tempted to view God's wise standards as archaic and the world's ways as more appropriate to our times.

Do you see the danger? Can you identify with the struggle? Then ponder the dangerous conflict our children face. Most of their values have not been tested and affirmed, proven and practiced as have yours and mine. They don't yet have the knowledge needed to discern error. Yet they face an incredible onslaught of counterfeit messages.

The Minds Behind the Movies

The *Star Wars* epics put America in touch with "the force." Their thrilling cosmic power struggle mesmerized millions, inspiring dreams of connecting with the same power system. Few bothered to examine the source of that "force."

The appealing images and visions of contemporary movies bombard our children, making them doubt God and seek "better" ways to power-living. Many young people create an imaginary world that seems more real and exciting than true reality. Quick to believe that nothing is impossible for man, viewers grasp for illusive dreams of space conquests, time travel, promiscuity without consequences, and connection with higher beings.

In *The Empire Strikes Back*, Yoda employs the "good side" of the force to raise Luke Skywalker's spaceship out of the swamp, showing his spellbound audience that man can accomplish anything he wants through faith in the "god of forces" (Daniel 11:38, KJV).

The mentality and worldview of people today are shaped more by imagery and attitudes from movies and TV than by values of religious and cultural tradition. The rise and development of the so-called "New Age Movement" is evidence of that fact. (Spiritual Counterfeits Project, Berkeley, California)

Visions and values taught in movies are not accountable to truth and reality. They are accepted, not on the basis of reason but because they excite the emotions, challenge the imagination, entice human nature, and manipulate minds.

The mind-set behind the media shows up in three studies by the research team of Lichter and Rothman. The column "News Media" represents views of the elite who influence major newspaper, magazine, and television news reporting. "TV Elite" represents those who write, select, and control television entertainment. "Movie" represents Hollywood's successful moviemakers.[1]

In *The Home Invaders*, Donald Wildmon warns:

These studies confirm the fact that the vast majority of leaders of both the national news media and the entertainment media are overtly hostile to the Christian faith. . . .

To the humanist mind and mentality, all influence of Christian faith must be removed from society. To achieve this end, the hu-

Attitude on Social Issues	News Media	TV Elite	Movie
Woman has right to decide on abortion	90%	97%	96%
Strongly agree homosexuality is wrong	9	5	7
Strongly agree homosexuals should not teach in public schools	3	6	4
Strongly agree adultery is wrong	15	16	13
Government should redistribute income.....	—	69	59
Government should reduce income gap	68	—	—
Government should guarantee jobs	48	45	38
Structure of society causes alienation	49	62	62
Institutions need overhaul	28	43	51

Religious Orientation	News Media	TV Elite	Movie
Jewish....................................	23%	59%	62%
Protestant	20	25	—
Catholic	12	12	—
Religion "none"	50	44	55
Seldom or never attend worship	86	93	96

Attitude Toward TV Entertainment	News Media	TV Elite	Movie
TV should promote social reform	—	66%	67%
Strongly agree that TV is too critical of traditional values	—	1	1

manist feels obligated and duty-bound to use whatever methods available, particularly the media.[2]

Crushing Christianity

You may remember when major movie studios produced biblical spectaculars such as *Ben Hur* and *The Ten Commandments.* Back then, movies honored our Christian heritage and God's ministers were portrayed as kind, wise, and faithful. Not anymore. Today, ministers are portrayed as foolish or corrupt. Followers of religion appear wimpy, immature, and out of touch with the real world. While most Americans call themselves Christians, they laugh along with the world at the biased portrayal of the church.

Hollywood not only demeans Christianity, but seems terrified of its influence. Look at the PG rating it gave Billy Graham's movie, *The Prodigal.* Usually, PG means that a movie contains enough sex, violence, or profanity to warrant a warning to parents. But these three factors were absent in *The Prodigal.* The real reason for the warning was to protect children against a dangerous religion: "Preteenage children should not be exposed to Christianity without their parents' consent."[3]

The anti-Christian bias, so visible through movies and television, shows an incredible double standard. Other religions apparently are safe and acceptable, but Christianity alone is judged dangerous and must be eliminated. Yet when Christians voice concern about immorality and violence, the angry media cries, "Censors!"

The furor surrounding *The Last Temptation of Christ* left no doubt about Hollywood's hostility toward Christianity. In choosing a story by Nikos Kazantzakis, it popularized the Greek novelist's philosophy—a contemporary blend of Buddhism, Lenin, Christ, Spinoza, Darwin, and Nietzsche—and gave birth to a mythological Jesus, who like other man-made gods, suits this present time. Like the gods of ancient Greece and Rome, this Jesus portrays the weaknesses of human nature rather than the triumph of spiritual obedience.

To Kazantzakis, God was the sum total of consciousness in the universe, expanding through human evolution. Even back in 1927, he envisioned a union of higher, evolved individuals with paranormal power, who were joined in a superhuman effort to create for themselves a new world.[4]

A student editorial for the Mountain View High School newspaper on October 12, 1988 said: "The controversial film, *The Last Temptation of Christ,* has been condemned and boycotted by many religious people. Their religious ignorance has made them scorn a movie they probably have not seen. If more of these misguided people watched this movie, they might actually approve of it. The film is powerful, gripping, beautiful, and very much on a human level. . . ."

It's far easier to identify with a confused, fallible, questioning Jesus than to accept the biblical Jesus' challenge to trust God for victory over sin. Discipline, self-denial, and the cross have no place in a society where "humanness" has become a virtue, where Self reigns as God, and where people are evolving into the "world's highest creators."

Angry that Christians would resist Hollywood's myth-making, Jack Valenti, president of the Motion Picture Association, declared, "[The] only issue is whether . . . self-appointed groups can prevent a film from being exhibited to the public or a book from being published. . . . "[5] In response, columnist Patrick Buchanan asked a question worth our contemplation:

> *Would Mr. Valenti defend a film titled* The Secret Life of Martin Luther King, Jr. *that depicted the assassinated civil rights leader as a relentless womanizer—a point of view with more foundation in truth, and surely, less of a profanation than showing Jesus of Nazareth as a lusting wimp?*
>
> *Of course not.*
>
> *We live in an age where the ridicule of blacks is forbidden, where anti-Semitism is punishable by political death, but where Christian-bashing is a popular indoor sport; and films mocking Jesus Christ are considered avant-garde. . . .*
>
> *"Sensitivity" is supposed to have become the mark of the man of decency in modern American life. So we are told. A "sensitive" man does not repeat ethnic jokes; he does not abide insults to any minority. . . .*
>
> *Christians, however, America's unfashionable majority, may be mocked, their preachers may be parodied in books and on film; their faith may be portrayed as superstitious folly. And secular society, invoking the First Amendment, will rush to the defense of the defamers, not the defamed.*
>
> *The battle over "The Last Temptation" is one more skirmish in the century's struggle over whose values, whose beliefs shall be*

exalted in American culture, and whose may be derided and disparaged.[6]

Bad Is Good

By banishing Christian truth and values from the screen, Satan has cleared the way for counterfeit messages. Without God's standard, anything goes. The world watches as Hollywood presents good as bad, morality as boring, and evil as delightful. The three main thrusts we saw in education—counterfeit religion, counterfeit values, and a counterfeit world system illuminate movie screens across our nation.

☐ First, a new religious system is replacing Christianity—primarily a mixture of humanism, hedonism, hinduism, and occultism. Whether the beautiful or the ugly side of evil, it testifies to the respectability that cloaks the New Age movement.

In the mythological setting of *Willow*, which is threaded with biblical allusions, occult wonders, and macho prowess, George Lucas tells a new set of youngsters a familiar message: the force is with you. Now garbed in ancient sorcery rather than space-age light sabres, the cosmic force shines through ugly trolls, pretty pixies, good as well as evil witches, and a courageous dwarf called Willow. Notice the messianic thrust: "A baby girl is born whom the *prophets* declare will be the savior of the land, and evil Queen Bavmorda vows to destroy the child. She's discovered like Moses, in the bulrushes on the banks of a river by Willow Ufgood, a tiny Newlyn and aspiring sorcerer...."[7]

This spiritual medley accomplishes two of Satan's purposes. By identification with occult symbols and cultural myths, it weakens the Christian message. And the same association veils the counterfeit in an aura of traditional credibility.

☐ Second, you can't miss the counterfeit values. Violence, immorality, profanity, and lawlessness (lying, cheating, disrespect toward authority) are standard fare—even in children's movies. For example, *Who Framed Roger Rab-*

bit? which could have been a delightful family movie, was tainted with sexist humor, sadistic violence, and vulgar comments. And *Ferris Bueller's Day Off* shows our hero lying to his parents and deceiving his teachers so disarmingly that you want to forget the wrongs and admire his wit.

☐ Third, the globalist's vision of a transformed world takes many forms. Man wields psychic forces, races through time, crushes the boundaries of death, and connects with evolved extraterrestrials. Impossibilities become realities; for nothing is impossible to the imagination. *Field of Dreams, Star Trek,* and *Ghostbusters* all show transcendent powers that put real life to shame.

Notice how the mythological story, *Dark Crystal,* illustrates Hindu-based global oneness: The movie begins with a look at two dying species: the kind Mystics and evil Skeksis. Long ago, "in the age of oneness," when the radiant Crystal transmitted harmony to everyone, the two were joined. But damage to the Crystal divided good and evil into two opposing forces. The damage can only be reversed, if, the moment three suns align, the crystal's missing chip is replaced. There is no time to lose, for the three suns have almost reached alignment.

As in the computer game by the same name, Jen, the crystal's chosen healer, overcomes all obstacles with the help of astrology, mystical chanting, telepathy, clairvoyance, and other psychic tricks. Finally, just before the three suns are aligned, he drops the chip into place. The crystal lights up, energy flows, good and evil merge into one, and harmony returns to the land. The parting message from the perfected beings: ". . . we all are part of each other. Now we leave you the Crystal of Truth. Make your world in its light."

This pantheistic/new age message grows more disturbing when we remember that Jim Henson, who wrote, directed, and produced this movie, is also the mind behind the "Muppets"—the popular stars of Sesame Street as well as of three popular video movies.

The chart in this chapter reveals the hidden purpose behind the immoral messages and occult visions: social reform. Hollywood, like the educational establishment and media elites, has caught Satan's vision: Absolve people who turn against God, and justify an alluring lifestyle of sensual pleasure, spiritual misadventure, and readiness for a new permissive kind of world.

Loving Evil

An advertisement for the movie *The Unholy* said it well: "Evil has never been so irresistible ... or so deadly."

We might add, "or so prevalent." As the '80s come to a close, evil—that dark, ugly face of the occult that hides behind the beautiful, enticing masks of the New Age—now shows its ugly countenance everywhere. Children are learning to love its scary, grotesque faces.

A study by the International Coalition Against Violent Entertainment (ICAVE) found that two-thirds of U.S. movies were rated violent, and half of those had themes of horror, satanism, or the occult. The most common motive for the slaughter, horror, and violence was vengeance. Viewers learned that rampant destruction and killing is okay if it avenges a despicable offense.[8]

Notice how horror movies have changed with the times. In *Halloween 4: The Return of Michael Myers*, Michael evolves beyond a mere homicidal maniac. Reflecting today's fascination with human potential and supernatural power, he now appears with supernatural strength, while his fellow actors exhibit cartoonlike qualities such as falling off roofs without injury.

Did you see *Gremlins* some years ago? Promoted as a children's movie, it turned into a nightmare. Yet kids loved it. Typical of the New Age, the movie softened hearts with the bright, happy side of evil: a lovable and intelligent little Mugway called Gismo. But happiness turned to horror when Gismo's evil offsprings became an army of ugly, lizardlike, demonic gremlins who destroyed everything in their path.

A scene where the vicious gremlins pushed against a door—their horny claws and red, cruel eyes peeping out from the crack until Billy, the hero, pushed the door shut—brought back memories from my own life.

In my third year as a Christian, I knew little about "pulling down" demonic strongholds (2 Corinthians 10:3-5) and freeing the oppressed. But I had pondered the triumphs of Jesus and His disciples over demonic forces. I longed to know the secret of victory both in my own life and in the more intense struggles that seemed to crush others.

One day a church leader asked me to counsel a young, depressed mother. Trusting that God's wisdom would be sufficient in my weakness, I accepted. A few days later, Sue and I spent seven hours together seeking and applying God's answers for her guilt, anger, and confusion. When she finally went home, Sue was radiant.

But I heard terror in her voice when she called late that night. Her spiritual battle exceeded anything I had imagined. God flashed one question into my mind which I asked her, "Sue, have you been involved in the occult?"

Her answer raised goose pimples on my arms. "Yes," she sobbed, "I worshiped Satan for three years. . . . The name they gave me is the name I gave my daughter. . . . "

I heard myself telling Sue to return the next week. We needed to pray together for release from the demonic bondage and oppression. I didn't know how, but trusted God would show me. I knew He had promised conquering power for battling evil in His name.

The next day, God miraculously trained me for warfare through the timely phone call of a stranger. And three days later, on the day He scheduled, He set Sue free. But the battle wasn't completely over. Through Luke 11:24, God reminded me to be on guard, lest the "evil spirits" return.

Sue promptly began to memorize, meditate, and keep her mind filled with Scriptures, for she might be tested very soon.

Indeed, she was. Eight days after God freed her, she experienced an onslaught of incredible terror. That night Sue and I battled against the demonic forces that claimed a territory no longer theirs. The images she described to me were identical to the demonic gremlins pushing against the door in the movie.

"Horrible, ugly demons are pressing on my mind," she cried. "I'm trying to shut the door, but I can't. Their hideous eyes are staring at me. . . . I can't get away from those eyes. . . . Help me!"

After a twenty-hour battle, Sue shut the door for good—by faith—and the demons departed. During the following year, as Sue fed on a daily diet of biblical truth, God completed her healing. She joined a neighborhood Bible study and later became one of the leaders. God is faithful! He can set free anyone who turns to Him in faith and obedience!

We need to ask ourselves and our children: "Do we want to be entertained by the ghastly, demonic creatures so prevalent in movies, on television, in toys, and comic books? Can God's children delight in the symbols of darkness and still enjoy God's presence and protection? I believe not. Listen to His warning in Psalm 97:10: "Let those who love the Lord hate evil, for He guards the lives of His faithful ones and delivers them from the hand of the wicked." And remember, God has something far better in store for those who say no to evil in order to follow Him.

CHAPTER EIGHT
What Can Parents Do About Persuasion by Identification?

See to it that no one takes you captive through hollow and deceptive philosophy, which depends on human tradition and the basic principles of this world rather than on Christ. (Colossians 2:8)

"Mom, why can't I see *Beetlejuice?*

"We talked about that yesterday."

"I forgot what you said."

Sandy felt exasperated. She didn't like to tell Tim that some of the movies "all" his friends enjoyed were out of bounds for him. Yet, she just couldn't ignore certain standards. They had debated this issue all the way home from school yesterday, and she felt too weary to take up the challenge again today.

"Mom, where does the Bible say that I can't see *Beetlejuice?*" Tim wasn't ready to accept no as an answer.

Sandy glanced at her son as she pulled away from the curb. His wide, blue eyes expressed sincere questioning, not rebellious disagreement. She knew he wanted to follow God's way but thought it sometimes seemed just too narrow. He hated to be different from everybody else.

"Help me, God," she prayed silently, then took a deep breath and began.

"Tim, the Bible doesn't mention *Beetlejuice* any more than it mentions rock music or crack. But God does make it very clear to us what He likes and what He hates. If you choose to do things He hates, it becomes harder and harder to choose to walk with God. You lose your sense of what is right, and you rationalize wrongs. Then you begin to think like those who don't know God—based on what *you* want, rather than what God wants."

"But how do you know God hates *Beetlejuice?*"

"We saw the advertisements, remember? I have talked with some people who have seen it. So have you." She glanced at him again, and saw the telltale look of reluctant assent. "Remember the Bible verses we looked up yesterday that show us what God thinks about spiritism, spells, and those kinds of things?"

"But everybody else gets to see stuff like that ..."

"You're different. You belong to God. Therefore, you can't do what everybody else does."

"Nothing happens to the kids who see those movies."

"Yes, it does. It just doesn't show right away. People can't watch all that corruption and not begin to change their attitude toward life and people. After a while, they can't tell the difference between right and wrong."

"I know the difference. Can't you trust me, Mom?" Tim sounded so confident that Sandy almost laughed.

"You asked me that last week, when you were choosing a video to take home. Remember the ones you wanted to see? In some areas of your life, you haven't yet shown that you have the wisdom to make wise choices. But I trust you to ride your bike safely into town and back."

It was Tim's turn to be silent.

"Tim, when we get home, I'll show you some passages in the Bible that will help you understand God's thoughts and teach you to be wise."

"God's thinking is very different from the way most people think, isn't it?" he asked thoughtfully.

"Nowadays it is," answered Sandy. She shivered as the awareness of the widening chasm between God's ways and the world hit her like an icy wind. "Precious Lord," she prayed silently, "help Tim choose Your ways, even when it means rejection and embarrassment. Teach him Your wisdom, so that He will want to choose Your way."

Sandy sensed both the danger of a movie's persuasive power and the need to teach her son discernment. She also experienced the frustration we feel when faced with a child we long to please as well as protect. How do we fulfill our responsibility in training a child in God's ways? Are our concerns grounded in reality? For answers, let's look again at the conflict.

The movie industry has amazing power. As a film forces viewers to make continual choices, it dulls their awareness of choosing, weakens their mental resistance to its pull, and becomes a persuasive tool for social change.

Marlin Maddoux, a Christian broadcaster and author of *America Betrayed,* speaks from his own experience within the media. He knows the plans of the media messengers as well as the vulnerability of millions of viewers.

> *We become enmeshed in it, unaware even of our surroundings, loving and hating the characters, making irrational judgments as to right or wrong, mesmerized by the genius of manipulation. . . .*
>
> *You are now at your highest point of vulnerability, and the authors and directors can now send you the "message" they want you to receive. . . . While you sit there in a passive, uncritical attitude, watching and listening, you have opened the door to almost total access to your subconscious mind. The media people know it—and they exploit it.[1]*

How do we help our children choose movies appropriate to their ages and faith? How do we prepare them to face the unexpected distortion they surely will encounter—even in a "good" movie? How can we encourage them to follow God's way, when it means saying "no"?

Step One: Finding the Right Movie

How do we find "safe" movies for our children? Are there any? Checking each possible choice personally would be a time-consuming torture. And the present rating system has failed to keep up with the changing film content. Introduced in 1968, it merely follows the shifting standards which slip further and further away from God's.

This relaxed rating system doesn't warn us that behind an innocent-sounding title and a PG rating hides a torrent of four-letter words and phrases. Today's rating system

Midnight Caller was an X-rated film . . . twenty years ago. Would it be an X today? No, I don't believe that for one moment. (Jack Valenti, Motion Picture Association of America)

doesn't reveal that sending our teenager to a PG-13 movie exposes him to sex scenes that signaled an R rating just a few years ago. And there's no warning of the assault on Christianity, the promotion of counterfeit religions, or the ghoulish, grotesque images so popular today.

The movie industry, which seems to lure younger and younger moviegoers with promises of forbidden fruit, opposes any modification of what might be called "obfuscation in labeling." It apparently fears that if parents are made aware in advance of some of the garbage their kids are exposed to, they might crack down and keep their children at home. (Cal Thomas, syndicated columnist and guest host on *Crossfire*)

God's answer for our family came in the form of a bimonthly bulletin called *Movieguide.* Published by Ted Baehr, it rates and evaluates current films according to quality and content—and, most importantly, from a biblical perspective. You can order *Movieguide* from Good News Communications, Inc., P.O. Box 9952, Atlanta, GA 30319.

Step Two: Be Prepared

☐ Pray together for continued wisdom and direction.
☐ Agree ahead of time to *leave* if the movie turns out to be worse than expected.
☐ Research the subject. Discuss biblical events or principles that relate to the movie's vision. For example, it deals with a futuristic, New Age kind of utopia, present the biblical view of the future.

☐ Be ready ahead of time to view counterfeit messages from a Christian perspective. Before seeing *Field of Dreams* with a friend, our fourteen-year-old read newspaper reviews and *Movieguide*. He went fortified with the following questions, which we discussed after when we met the boys for ice cream.

–Why does the movie make people "feel good"?

–Where does it sound like Christianity but contradict the Bible?

–What did it say or imply about God, His values, or heaven?

–Did you see anything supernatural? What was its source—God or Satan?

☐ Put on the whole armor of God. If we go to enjoy a movie without the armor—without choosing to count on truth as our filter, the life of Jesus as our righteousness, and faith in our Shepherd as our shield—we will begin to absorb some of the movie's counterfeit values. We will be allowing the world to squeeze us into its mold.

But remember, if we go somewhere God does not want us to go, His armor will not protect us from the consequences. We can't put on the "breastplate of [God's] righteousness"—which assumes our assent to His will—then go our own way rather than His.

It is essential to understand what God does and does not promise to do. If I presume that God's protection extends beyond His promise, I will become disappointed and frustrated. The truth is that His armor may or may not protect me against the storms of the world (Matthew 5:45). But it will always protect me against the assaults of Satan, whose arrows use the circumstances of the world to crush and destroy far more than could any storm.

In other words, God may not take me out of my circumstances, but He will bring victory in the midst of the trial. He will protect me against discouragement, despair, hopelessness, worthlessness—all the destructive emotions and thought patterns that rise up inside to disturb my peace, deny my resources in Christ, and quench my joy in Him.

I learned that lesson the hard way. During my first three years as a Christian, I worked with the chaplain's service in a local VA hospital. Both patients and chaplains encouraged me to attend a "new, transforming" group therapy session, which had "freed them up" to relate to others with more love and transparency. Curious and open to adventure, I went.

The session didn't impress me. I heard nothing new, only the same profanity I had been exposed to on other days. But something changed *in* me. Suddenly God seemed distant and my mind seemed out of tune with His.

Later I realized why. My Lord had not sent me. I went to the session to satisfy my own curiosity, to please others, and to gain knowledge that opposed His truth. Because I failed to protect my mind, the profanity I heard found entrance and gained a foothold. For the next three months, four-letter words would burst into my thoughts. Daily I begged that God would cleanse and renew my mind. When the onslaught ended, I had learned my lesson. When I go where my Shepherd sends me, no evil can drive a wedge between Him and me. But if I choose my own way, no matter how much I affirm the armor, I suffer the consequences.

Step Three: Others Go, But You Cannot

As parents, sometimes you just have to say no. It's hard! Your child's friends will all talk about a popular show which he alone missed. You hurt with him and wish you could shield him from the pain—but you cannot without compromising your faith. Suffering for Christ's sake is an unavoidable part of a disciple's life. You just hope to see the pain produce wisdom and maturity rather than bitterness and rebellion. How can you encourage him?

A good video, a trip to the ball game, and other distractions can help. But only God's Word can change his attitude, bring wisdom, and produce maturity.

The following Scriptures will deepen his understanding of what it means to be a Christian. You may want to choose a Scripture each morning, then discuss it at a predetermined time later in the day.

As you read the Scripture passages, ask yourself these questions: What does it say? What is God saying *to me?* How can I apply it to my life?

☐ Look at what God wants to accomplish.
-James 1:2-4
-Romans 5:3-5
-1 Peter 5:6-10

☐ Listen to what God tells you to avoid.
-Romans 12:9
-Ephesians 4:17-20
-Deuteronomy 18:10-13

☐ Know that God has wonderful plans for those who follow Him.
-Matthew 5:11-12, 13-16
-Romans 8:16-18
-2 Corinthians 4:16-18

The object of our focus changes our lives. When we focus on immorality and violence, these mental pictures mold our thinking and behavior. But when we focus on God and His truth, He fills us and makes us more like Himself. The transformation the world offers can't compare to what God promises His children.

We, who with unveiled faces all reflect the Lord's glory, are being transformed into His likeness with ever-increasing glory, which comes from the Lord, who is the Spirit. (2 Corinthians 3:18)

SUGGESTED READING

Home Invaders by Donald E. Wildmon
America Betrayed by Marlin Maddoux

CHAPTER NINE
Television and Mind Manipulation

Television is first and foremost an educational medium. It is an instrument of persuasion, indoctrination, seduction, propaganda, and mind manipulation—all done in an entertaining way. (Marlin Maddoux)

"I am God! I am God! I AM GOD!"

The staggering claim Shirley MacLaine had shouted to the ocean waves was suddenly echoing through America's homes. The charming star of the New Age was coaching fifty million prime time viewers in self-realization. Her 1987 testimony bore an ominous likeness to Satan's original lie: just transcend the limits of past religious conditioning and share the journey toward God-ness.

Having affirmed her personal divinity, MacLaine seeks "higher truths" from Hindu Avatars and channeled spirit guides. Etheric beings like "John," "Ramtha," and "Lazaris" seem delighted to teach her their philosophies. Soon she is ready for her next step—a trip to the Peruvian Andes.

Near ancient Machu Picchu—supposedly a favorable cli-

One condition for the widespread acceptance of the occult is that it must first attain an image of neutrality and innocence. *Out on a Limb* laid the foundation for that image change overnight. No one seemed to notice that deep cultural and spiritual values had been glibly reversed in the process. (Spiritual Counterfeits Project)

---

mate for UFOs and psychic energies—MacLaine gives a
soaring demonstration of astral travel. After rejoining her
body, she receives second-hand guidance from "Mayan," a
beautiful extraterrestrial. Not only does "Mayan's" wisdom
and psychic power outshine any earthling's, but this alien
genuinely cares about man's plight and wants to help. So
she commissions Shirley to be a New Age teacher to this
ignorant world—an assignment wholeheartedly accepted.

MacLaine's endorsement of mysticism sparked sales of
every kind of occult and metaphysical literature—especially her own books. To thousands of more serious converts,
channeling and connecting with "Higher Selves" became
household hobbies. But few outside the Christian community recognized her religion for what it really was: ancient
occultism wearing an enchantingly beautiful mask.

Energized by the kind of exposure only television could
provide, the New Age movement had burst into the mainstream, kindled American imaginations and accelerated the
social transformation begun by humanist reformers.

Television writers and producers took note of its enticing themes: Be God, take control, don't let out-dated religious values hinder your self-discovery, follow your feelings, wield the Force and create a world of peace and love.
Whether subtle or overt, soon all these facets of New Age
beliefs had invaded family and children's programs.

To understand how it happened, look again at the
Lichter and Rothman study in chapter 7. It suggests that
men and women who have rejected God and His values
now determine what Americans watch on television: Two
out of three media leaders "believe that TV entertainment
should be a major force for social reform. This is perhaps
the single most striking finding in our study. According to
television's creators, they are not in it just for the money.
They also seek to move their audience toward their own
vision of the good society."[1]

Even news is shown through the filters of media biases.
How can we believe what we see, when actors may be
used to "show" an action that never was filmed? Or when
broadcasters emphasize or cut news items to fit their
views?

During the political conventions of 1988, our family waited in front of the television set to hear the views of party leaders. It looked promising. The networks had scheduled several hours of live coverage each day. But after the first evening, we felt betrayed. Instead of firsthand reports, we saw teasing glimpses. In fact, endless discussions of *personal observations, interpretation, and opinions* blocked our view of the candidates.

What kind of values guide this movement? For networks, squeezed by competition from cable, independent stations, and videos—whatever sells! During a debate with Donald Wildmon, Gene Mater, a vice president of CBS, exposed his position: "Mr. Wildmon is a minister and has a stated set of values. I am a broadcaster and I don't."[2]

Teaching That Transforms

No one disputes television's power to teach and model godly values and useful skills to generations of children. Experience has proven its effectiveness. For example, in one *Happy Days* episode, Fonzie gets a library card. Soon afterward, libraries across the country reported a noticeable rise in the number of children requesting cards.

[Only] the TV machine . . . holds such a devastating potential for brainwashing, mass programming, and the destruction of individualism—with, of course, reinforcement from the other mass media. This threat is every bit as disastrous for the future of mankind as is pollution, overpopulation, or atomic and biological warfare.[4]
(Wilson Bryan Key in *Subliminal Seduction*)

Television wields the same potential for modeling profanity, promiscuity, permissiveness, and counterfeit power. We have seen both the good and the bad, but in the tug of war between two forces, the latter is winning by a landslide.

"It used to be that children didn't understand much of the adult world until they were old enough to read about it in books," observes Dr. William Dietz, chairman of the American Academy of Pediatrics Subcommittee on Children and Television. "With the advent of television, children are exposed to more sophisticated messages at earlier ages."[3]

What then does television teach our children? The spectrum is broad and varied. But let's look at key categories and consider how the media message molds young minds.

☐ Laugh at religion. Whether they like it or not, media leaders can't ignore Christian memorials like Christmas, but they can exclude Christ. By secularizing Christian holidays and laughing at ineffective representatives from the church, they display a lifeless, inept, and materialistic substitute—which is not Christianity at all.

Marlin Maddoux writes, "Humor . . . is one of the best ways to get past a person's defenses. Then, when these defenses are down, the 'messages' can be sent straight to the subconscious mind where it will be stored to eventually affect the thinking and lifestyle of the subject."[5]

☐ If it feels good, do it. Prime-time sitcoms, soaps, miniseries, and mysteries model a passionate medley of yesterday's sexual and spiritual taboos, for this is the "liberated generation"—hopelessly addicted to entertainment.

Profanity, crudity, sarcasm, and cynicism spice up the action. Have you noticed how quickly children have added this new peppery flavor to their conversations and humor? Kindness doesn't fit unless it serves self-interest, but impudence is cool. Respect for parents is downright embarrassing, but following your own rules earns peer respect—or at least appreciative laughter.

☐ Experiment with magic. The bright, beautiful gods and

Failure to rally around a set of values means that we are turning out highly skilled barbarians. (Dr. Steven Muller, president of Johns Hopkins University) dark, cruel gods both draw power from a single source. So when Papa Smurf conquers evil with magical charms or when Teddy Ruxpin's friends trust in the divining power of crystals, or if the CareBears transform their world with loving vibes, they are all teaching counterfeit spirituality.

Thousands of children watched the young Houdini perform magic not by illusions, but through a force that he learned from a wise, old Indian shaman.

Others saw Hooperman seeking help from a frustrated channeler to solve a murder. The last scene showed the police chief, who at first resented involvement with the supernatural, sneaking a visit to the triumphant psychic.

A Smurf episode shows Mother Earth guiding the forces of nature with her magic wand. When her wand breaks, an earthquake frees a wizard determined to steal the smurf's eternal-life stone. In the end, good magic conquers evil, the wand is restored, and the earth healed.[6]

Magic, packaged for every age, prepares youngsters to accept occult forces without questioning their source. Appealing to their desire for secret knowledge and power to control their world, the supernatural has infiltrated almost every kind of program—including ads.

□ Pursue a new world order. With television, mass programming has become a chilling reality. Media spokesmen wield power to censor facts, select information, ridicule vital principles, build illusive expectations, and direct America's thinking. Today's information glut has produced an audience ill-equipped to argue with the "experts."

Some years ago, the late Dr. Francis Schaeffer spoke at a National Religious Broadcasters' convention. Marlin Maddoux summarized some of his key points:

My clear impression, received from Dr. [Francis] Schaeffer's revelations, is that our nation is being systematically conditioned [by the media, public schools, and legislature] to accept a totalitarian, humanistic, elite ruling class. The rationale used for the concept of a one-world, all-powerful ruling class is that it is the only way to save the world from collapsing economically and socially.

This is the reasoning of the self-appointed social "elite" who feel they are the only ones who have the intelligence and power to prevent mankind from destroying itself. And, if in the process of saving the world they have to destroy the Constitution of the United States and the personal freedom and dignity of the American people, then so be it! The threat to the Constitution is very real.[7]

At the heart of the New Age vision is the conviction that humanity is poised between two ages. The perils of our time are interpreted not as the prelude to apocalyptic disaster [unless the "crisis" can serve as a persuasive tool], but evolutionary transformation. (Robert J.L. Burrows, Spiritual Counterfeits Project)

☐ **Don't hide from the horror.** Have Halloween's ghosts, ghouls, and goblins come to stay all year? It seems that way. "In an overview of three weeks of prime-time movies, not including cable networks, there were thirty-two movies that had either occult or satanic themes," reports Peter Lelonde, publisher of *The Omega Letter*.

"Just turn it off!" argue network spokesmen, refusing any responsibility for what viewers happen to see. One woman shared her response to this kind of simplistic advice in *U.S. News and World Report.*

My heart is palpitating. Sweat pops from my forehead. The chair clings to my body. Back-to-back sequences of supernatural carnage unfold before me. Unsuspecting young victims are wrenched with soul-shivering cries into a world of malignant forms, satanic demons, and evil incarnate. . . .

Each day's end brings terrifying commercial for yet another terrifying horror film. . . . Against my will I have become familiar with Jason of Friday the 13th and Freddy of Nightmare on Elm Street. Against my will, I've seen the faces of little children placed in the wake of sickness dredged from the depths of adult deviancy. . . .

I do not now, nor will I ever, deny others their right to fright. I am only asking that it not be forced upon me and my small children, who've learned to "duck for cover" while we wait for the black horror to pass. I agree to give you the spooky, the scary, the startling. In return, give me back my family viewing hours and let me nestle softly among those I love, free from fright.[8]

The Effect on Children

How does television influence our children's view of themselves and their environment? Consider these factors:

□ It replaces other activities. By 1984, the average television set was in use seven hours, two minutes each day. (The A.C. Nielsen Company)[9] Playing, reading, and studying had become unpleasant distractions to young TV addicts. Family games, reading, conversation, or other forms of social interaction—needed to build caring, responsive, and discriminating individuals—require more initiative and mental energy than many TV families are willing to exert.

Children cannot test the world they see in the television set. Newspapers and books allow time to stop, ponder, and ask questions. Not television. Since children's ability to evaluate messages can't keep up with TV's rapid action presentations, their learning is often passive and involves automatic acceptance.

□ It produces unreasonable demands and expectations. Commercials and ad cartoons like *My Little Pony* and *G.I. Joe* stimulate children's desires, or the advertisers wouldn't spend millions to persuade them to buy. Young children, unable to differentiate between a show and an ad, receive the exaggerated or deceptive sales pitch with the same trust that they listen to a parent or teacher.

"Television encourages the use of drugs, alcohol, and tobacco by glamorizing them. The heroes whom children emulate are often shown smoking and drinking beer." (American Academy of Pediatrics)[10]

□ It gives a distorted view of the world. Since children depend heavily on television to fill in gaps in their experience, they tend to accept what it tells them. The younger the child, the fewer facts he has for evaluating what he sees and hears. Therefore, the images presented on the screen help shape his perception of his world.

"Children up to age seven understand very little of the plot," says Charles Atkins, Telecommunications Professor at Michigan State University. "They identify closely with characters . . . and like watching them do things, even though they don't understand the big picture." In other words, a child might see a burglar break into a home in the first scene, and not connect this crime with the imprisonment shown twenty-five minutes later.[11]

□ It models harmful relationships. Television programs show adolescents how to relate to the opposite sex and produce a perverted concensus in their peer culture. Sexual promiscuity becomes a normal part of life, while the consequences—unwanted pregnancies, incurable sexually transmitted diseases, the inner torment of emotional bondings and breakups—rarely receive fair exposure.

A study by Michigan State University on media, teens, and sex found that "girls watching their favorite TV shows saw 1,500 sexual acts or references per year, boys viewed nearly 1,300. On average, girls watched TV for 5.6 hours a day, including at least two soap operas on weekdays. Boys watched 5.2 hours of TV per day."[12]

□ It models violent behavior. "Studies have linked violence on TV with aggressive behavior in children and adolescents," says pediatrician Victor Straburger, a consultant to the American Academy of Pediatrics Subcommittee on Children and Television. "One can't say for sure that a child will start a fire after watching a drama about arson, but the connection appears consistently throughout all kinds of studies."[13]

"By the time a child graduates from high school, he will have seen 18,000 killings on television."[14] Watching hours of painless "fantasy violence," children learn to view violence as a normal and acceptable way to express anger and handle conflicts. Even sexual violence loses its horror. Some are trapped in its deadly grip, as executed serial-killer Ted Bundy testified in an interview with Dr. James Dobson in January 1989:

> *The FBI's own study on serial homicide shows that the most common interest among serial killers is pornography. . . Dangerous impulses are being fueled day in and day out by violence in the media in its various forms, particularly sexualized violence. And what scares and appalls me, Dr. Dobson, is what I see on cable TV. Some of the violence in the movies that come into homes today is stuff that they wouldn't show in X-rated adult theatres thirty years*

ago. This stuff—I'm telling you from personal experience—is the
most graphic violence on screen, particularly as it gets into the
homes, to children who may be unattended or unaware that they
may be a Ted Bundy who has that vulnerability or predisposition
to be influenced by that kind of violence.[15]

☐ It produces fear. According to "The Foundation for
Child Development," children who are heavy TV watchers
were twice as likely to "get scared often."[16] No wonder!
While violence appears exciting on television, it presents a
frightening picture of the world we live in. Children store
in their minds vivid images of horrendous possibilities.
Families pay a high price for enjoying evil.

☐ It clouds discernment of right from wrong. The biblical attitudes of trust, obedience, and surrender clash with a
world where self reigns and values have turned upside
down. Again and again television presents an ominous reversal: Good is bad, and bad is good. In the Gospel message, confessing sin brings cleansing and the Cross sets us
free. Yet New Agers reject sin and the Cross as "negatives"
unfit for a new, "progressive" world system.

Oprah Winfrey illustrated this game of opposites in February 1988 when she hosted an unlikely pair: Dr. Aquino, a
high priest in the satanic temple of Seth, and Johanna
Michaelson who wrote *The Beautiful Side of Evil*. About
halfway through the program, Oprah turned to Johanna,
saying, "Dr. Aquino has told us that the satanism he represents is good, not evil. Is that possible?"

"Well it is," answered Johanna, "if you come from a
frame of mind where left is right, bad is good, black is
white, in is out, and upside down is right side up—which is
the basic approach of satanism. Everything is backwards.
So to him, satanism is good and everything else is bad.
That's his perspective. However, he is wrong!"

God warns us about this kind of manipulative make-
believe: "Woe to those who call evil good and good evil,
who substitute darkness for light and light for darkness,
who substitute bitter for sweet and sweet for bitter! Woe to
those who are wise in their own eyes and clever in their
own sight!" (Isaiah 5:20-21)

CHAPTER TEN

What Can Parents Do About Mind Manipulation?

I will walk in my house with blameless heart.
I will set before my eyes no vile thing.
The deeds of faithless men I hate;
  they will not cling to me. . . .
I will have nothing to do with evil. (Psalm 101:2-4)

"Please turn off the television, David."

"Why can't I see 'The Real Ghostbusters'?"

"Because it teaches kids to enjoy the occult, and because it makes man seem like God—able to control the forces of evil."

"All my friends watch it."

"David, you know how I feel about that argument. I don't want you to follow everyone else."

"But when Todd and Troy were my age, you let them see stuff like that. . . ."

"Times have changed. Some of the shows they watched—like 'The Munsters'—seemed so remote from reality. But today, kids can experiment with the very things that these cartoons suggest and model. . . . The occult wasn't such an obvious part of our world ten years ago. Today it is blatant. Especially on television."

"You never let me see anything!"

"That's not true. . . ."

I felt my son's frustration—and my own. Longing to offer him something good and fun, I prayed for direction in dealing with him.

Since we had this discussion some years ago, David has

learned to discern for himself. It didn't happen overnight; but with prayer, Bible study, practice, and a deepening commitment to follow truth, he is developing the habit of seeing and making choices about life from God's perspective.

Step One: Pray

□ Pray for wisdom to know what to watch, and self-control to abstain. Set a good example.

□ Pray for consistency in maintaining God's standards. Remember that even if your child knows and agrees with your values, a diet of deception, distortion, and evil will affect his perspective. He cannot enjoy what God hates and remain immune to being "hardened by sin's deceitfulness" (Hebrews 3:13).

□ Pray that no other hero overshadows the true God in your child's life. When identifying with television's idols, children can lose interest in and a sense of need for the God of the Bible. "What's so great about Him?" they wonder. "Does He lift skyscrapers and smash the bad guys with ray guns? Does He zoom through the air or explore outer space?"

We know that He who made earth and space can do all these and more—but from a child's limited perspective God often seems tame. The biblical stories cannot compete with cartoons in the action-packed stimulation many children have learned to crave.

□ Pray for appropriate guidelines for television viewing.

Step Two: Affirm God's Values Together

□ Continue family Bible study.

□ Discuss these questions: What do you remember best from a movie or television program—the good values or the shocking violence? What do you forget? What could help you remember the good things and overlook evil? If you are watching a show which suddenly pictures immoral, violent, or occult scenes, do you find it difficult to turn it off? What does that tell you about the subtle appeal of evil?

☐ Discuss news reports and other information. Is all of it true or might there be distortions? Remember, a democracy cannot succeed unless its people are informed with facts. Finding the truth in the midst of all the editorializing is work. But work we must, or the media will mold our thinking.

Will Rogers, the great student of Americana, once said, "All I know is what I read in the papers." If Will were around today, no doubt he would have contemporized that statement to, "All I know is what I see on television." More people can see than can read, and today they are seeing it more than ever before—on television. (Jane Chastain)[1]

The late scholar Joseph Campbell profoundly affected millions who watched him dialogue with Bill Moyers on public television. Charming and articulate, Campbell viewed Christianity as merely one myth among the many— and far less appealing than some. He often validated his conclusions by "quoting the Bible." Only those who knew God's Word well enough to discern error—or took time to check each reference—could recognize the distortions in his use of the Bible.

☐ Find videocassettes that model God's values, teach Bible stories, or tell a heartwarming story without profanity, immorality, or New Age overtones. Check your local Christian bookstore. They may carry rental videos that both entertain as well as testify to God's greatness through the lives of His people.

☐ List programs or movies seen during the past week. Discuss the values they taught or demonstrated. Don't just say "This is bad" or "This is good." Be specific. Give reasons. This helps your child appreciate and remember what is true and reject what is false.

Step Three: Train Your Child to Discern Deception

Challenge your child to be a scout for God—one who notices every message that wars against His truth. Train him to ask himself these questions:

☐ Does it picture obscenity, nudity, sex, cruelty, and violence? Watch for the subtle as well as the obvious—images tucked into sweet stories or flashed into a cartoon. For example, Bugs Bunny found a magic lamp with a genie who could fulfill his wishes. Bugs' last wish: transport into a sultan's harem.

Because kids see so much "fantasy violence"—which involves no pain, suffering, or long-term recuperation—aggression may appear to be an acceptable, even normal way to express frustration and handle conflict.[2]

☐ Does one or more of the characters play the role of God? Do some of these gods, such as He-man and Superman, seem greater and more real than God? Or does the story suggest that each person is a god, the designer and creator of his own circumstances? Does it imply each person has power within himself to overcome all obstacles and fulfill his dreams?

☐ Does the winning side draw on power not from God? If supernatural power is not from God, it is demonic. Some years ago, this may have seemed less important in society, but today, as psychic phenomena and demonic power are becoming a normal, acceptable part of American life, we must guard our children's minds from absorbing this lie and forgetting its danger. Constant exposure tends to bring unquestioning acceptance, so be careful.

Like the graceful, hypnotic dance of the cobra, New Age spirituality is the beautiful, seductive side of evil—and it's deadly!

☐ Does good win over evil? Does it show your child that there are consequences for violating God's standards? They may show consequences for violating the world's values, yet reward those who violate God's. For example, one cartoon showed Woody Woodpecker demonstrating all his nasty ways to avenge an offense and get away with it.

□ Do you hear references to New Age phrases such as "higher intelligence," "past lives" (reincarnation), "mind evolution," and "perfection" through magic and counterfeit powers. These are rampant in many space fantasies.

□ Does it emphasize occult power? Are sorcery, spells, clairvoyance, divination, and other psychic formulas presented as helpful tools to successful living? Might it produce curiosity or fascination with the occult and a desire to experiment? These demonic traps are far more deadly than drugs or alcohol. Our God hates these things; how, then, can His children enjoy them?

□ Does it pass the test of Philippians 4:8? "Whatever is true ... noble ... right ... pure ... lovely ... think about such things." Write a list of programs that encourage kindness, helpfulness, and respect for others. Share them with others.

Step Four: Join the Battle for Truth

What kind of examples do we, their parents, set? Do we dare let the power that opposes everything that God is and does, be a source of entertainment for us?

□ Speak up about pornography, sexually explicit scenes, vulgarity, profanity, violence, and the occult. A silent church is likely to be a compromising church. If we don't hold each other and our leaders accountable, we can all too easily buy into the media message.

□ Write advertisers of objectionable shows. Since they want to gain, not lose customers, they welcome your opinion. The networks, in turn, respond to complaints from their advertisers. The American Family Association, founded by the Reverend Donald Wildmon, keeps records of TV advertisers. Write for information at P.O. Box 2440, Tupelo, MS 38803.

One evening Fox Television's "Married ... with Children" pictured a woman removing her bra. Dressed only in her briefs and a garter belt, she asked two men, "How do you think I look?" Terry Rakolta, a Michigan mother, happened to be watching. Appalled at the "blatant exploitation of women, sex, and anti-family attitudes," she wrote to the show's advertisers, urging them to cancel their support. Fifteen sponsors responded with genuine concern and promised to either drop the show or review future episodes.

In fact, the results were so astounding that in the ensuing months, Rakolta appeared on various news and talk shows. But the praise was far from unanimous. Verbalizing the media's general view of those who dare speak up for Christian values, the Los Angeles Times labeled her a "right wing fundamentalist," "half crazed," and in the "lunatic fringe." The cost of being counted as Jesus' disciple is rising.[3]

The real issue . . . is far greater than sex and violence on television. At stake is the very foundation on which Western civilization is built.[4]

☐ Pray that God would show your family His concerns so that you can battle in prayer as you watch various shows. When Jimmy Owens, the author of the musical *If My People*, watches network news, he prays. "It has become my most intense time of intercession each day," he told the editor of *Intercessors For America (IFA)* "How often have we said, 'Wouldn't it be wonderful if we had a way to call multitudes of intercessors to immediate alert on subjects of great urgency?' All along we have had it—right in our living room."[5]

God tells us—children and parents alike—to be "wise as serpents and innocent as doves" (Matthew 10:16). That means we must be alert to what is happening, see all things from His perspective, resist any compromise with the evil around us, and let God use us to accomplish His purpose.

CHAPTER ELEVEN

Toys and Games and Distortions of Imagination

Children project themselves with their imagination into a toy. They give it life, character, abilities, and talents and set the surrounding around it. This is how they learn. (Phil Phillips in Turmoil in the Toy Box*)*

Toy stores are safe, happy places. Right? Some are. But many have traded treasured age-appropriate toys for glamor dolls and occult warriors that catapult even young children into the world of adult conflicts.

The macho, magical, and macabre have captivated children for ages. *Grimm's Fairy Tales* filled my own childhood in Norway with images of wicked, spell-casting witches and three-headed trolls who turned children into stone. The tales were fun, exciting, and *obviously unreal.*

Today's acceptance of counterfeit forces has made the mystical grimly *real.* By itself, a fairy tale or toy will hardly shape a child's attitudes. But reinforced by school, movies, music, and television, the combined messages generate tolerance and acceptance of the demonic.

My childhood toys freed my imagination to direct the play. I—not the toymaker—assigned personalities and feelings to my toys and interacted with them according to my understanding of the world around me.

Those traditional toys, if still available, fade in the glamorous light of toys that star in movies, cartoons, and comic books. Complete with built-in personalities, these new playmates both stifle and steer the imagination. G.I. Joe and the Ghostbusters have been outfitted for battle—nothing else. The play naturally moves in that one direction.

When a child watches a cartoon and then plays with a toy connected to that cartoon, he is no longer projecting himself into the toy. Instead, cartoons have programmed the child to play with toys in a certain way. (Phil Phillips in *Turmoil in the Toybox*)

Whether smiley or scary, dolls and action figures come to life through a child's imagination. Through their good or evil characteristics, they teach about life and relationships. As the child plays, he acts out his growing (and often distorted) perception of his world, validating and strengthening the message behind the toy. John Dvorak, writing for the *San Francisco Examiner*, asks:

> *When trying to understand the mood of the country, its future, and its direction, where do you turn?*
>
> *Many journalists follow the annals of Congress; others have deep discussion with learned professors. I go to Toys R Us. Here's where the forthcoming generations are molded. Let me tell you, the future die is cast and the image is a sick one. It's not that the toy business hasn't always been fraught with weird fads, tasteless imagery, and warped symbols that have little value. But now it's worse than ever. One is simply overwhelmed by a plethora of toys best described as gruesome, gory, and irresponsible.[1]*

A Wonderland of Dreams and Magic

Join me on a hair-raising journey through a modern fantasyland—the local toy store. You will meet aliens, demons, ghosts, and goblins. You will see horrendous humanoids, scary supernaturals, haunted humans, and shimmering seductive dolls. You will discover video games that equip *you* with mystical power and pit you against diabolical forces.

Grab a cart, and we'll start by the left wall of the cavernous showroom. Scanning the endless display of unfamiliar games—undoubtedly many good ones—your eyes rest momentarily on *Shriefs and Creeks* and *Eternia*—the homeland of the Masters of the Universe. Then, near a stack of Ouija Boards, you spot *Therapy*, which promises "fascinating fun with a psychological twist." To the true-or-false question, "Playing hard to get definitely works," it answers: "False. Males . . . tend to need encouragement. The most popular girls are open with their emotions, not guarded."

Across from the board games stretches the formidable wall of electronic and computer games. *Nintendo* sounds familiar, so you stop to examine its display. You breathe a sigh of relief at the sight of good old themes like Sesame Street, Mickey Mouse, and football. But other pictures jump out at you—strange aliens, shrewd sorcerers, hideous demons, fiery dragons. You quickly move on.

The end wall displays books. You notice a "deluxe" color/activity book called *Masters of the Universe*. Browsing through its pages you see a story that little children can color: "The Snake Pit—Join HE-MAN as he rescues BATTLE CAT from the SNAKE MEN and foils the evil plan of SKELETOR!" You scan "Slimy Rescue!" "Laser Messages," "Castle Ghoulies," and "Mirror Magic Mazes."

The four-page posters picture "He-Man in the Blasterhawk Battle and Skeletor in the Fright Fighter!" Skeletor, the "Lord of Destruction," controls the dark side of the force. His head is a skull and he carries a ram's head staff, two symbols of death and satanism. You wonder how a little boy could sleep with that awful picture on his wall.

You move down an aisle of guns of every shape and kind, from *Neutra-Laser*, which fires invisible infrared beams, to *Glooper*, which fires "globs of oozing, slimy gloop up to 25 feet." A delight to clean up, no doubt.

Turning the corner you almost stumble into the *Mad Scientist* with lures such as "Dissect An Alien" or "Yank Out Alien Organs Dripping in Glowing Alien Blood."

In the next two aisles you find armies of action figures you recognize from television cartoons. First you spot the *Teenage Mutant Ninja Turtles*, the strange, green humanoid turtles that topped the popularity lists in 1989. Turtles?

They look more like musclemen with snake heads.

Next, the *Thundercats* come with *Mumm-Ra's Tomb Fortress*, where skeletal Mumm-Ra "mystically" transforms into MUMM-RA THE EVERLIVING. Two dragon-tailed Man/Beast (mutants) "Statue Guardians" guard the skull-shaped transformation chamber.

You notice you have entered the occult section of the store, for after Sharkoss, Demon of the Deep from "The Other World" waits Mattel's "Masters of the Universe." The blond, handsome He-Man and glamorous She-Rah contrast starkly with the grotesque creatures all around them. The largest boxes contain the skull-shaped "Castle Grayskull," He-Man's home in "Eternia" and the source of his power.

"The Real Ghostbusters" offers a personal *Ghostzapper* along with the ghost you want: Ecto-2, Gooper Ghost, Sludge Bucket, Green Wolf—even a Haunted Human if you like. You stare in amazement at Sweet Old Granny who changes into Granny Gross. Her jaw drops down to reveal vampire teeth and a long, extended tongue, while her hat lifts up to expose a second forehead with a third eye.

By the time the child is a teen, unless his parents have instilled Christian values in him, he will have more knowledge of the occult than he will have of God. (Phil Phillips in *Turmoil in the Toybox*)

Even *Nintendo* provides action figures to match its games. One box shows a white mummy-like figure attacking the mighty hero Link. Like a growing number of contemporary action toys, it comes with a short, enticing history that ties an occult myth to a more believable reality.

Two aisles down you find the soft toys. There's a talking *Alf* with some other alien-life forms. There's PeeWee's green dragonish *Pet Pterri* and a purple *Wooly What's It.* But what happened to the old-fashioned teddy bears? These cuddlies have devilish horns, huge lionlike teeth, or chains around their necks. Some have two wild, distorted eyes, others have just one. No question about it—these bright colored, velvety creatures are monsters!

You head for the dolls. "Be cool!" shouts dazzling Dolly, one of the "Hollywoods." Does cool mean makeup for little girls? The number of little cosmetic cases suggests it. The pink cases contrast sharply with the Halloween makeup on the same shelf. Instead of a pretty face, try one with gray, ghostly skin, bloody streaks, and ghoulish scars.

You're leaving, and on the way out you glimpse Play-doh. Ah, there's a good safe toy! But wait, this Play-doh box wears the title "The Real Ghostbusters—Glow-in-the-Dark Play-doh." You don't even have to form your own imagined ghosts and monsters. Play-doh does it for you!

What Do They Teach?

Toys can help children learn to solve problems, share ideas, express frustation, use their imagination, develop creativity, and concentrate on a project. But these benefits can be misused. We have seen how counterfeit teaching touches our children through schools, movies, and television. The messages from toys fall into the same three categories: altered religion, values, and world system.

□ A counterfeit religion. Children have learned that ghosts and demons yield to the Ghostbusters' mightier power. The cartoon stories prove that nothing is impossible for them. Humanism (belief in man's infinite capacity) plus New Age power raise these four ghostbuster heroes—and anyone who identifies with them—to spiritual mastery.

Where then is God?

The toy/cartoon linkup commands a strong influence. The child bases his play on the story; lacking a strong enough belief-system of his own, he incorporates the fiction into his life. Whether he visualizes himself as G.I. Joe using his power to defeat his enemies, or as a Ghostbuster subduing demonic spirits, a child plays according to Satan's original lie: You will not surely die . . . you will be like God" (Genesis 3:4).

This enticing illusion fires a child's heart with delicious dreams that lure him away from truth. In time, the child outgrows the vision but grasps greedily for the next one that the deceiver dangles. That next vision might come through video games. In *Super Mario Brothers 2*—which is less occult-centered than many other popular videos—*you* are Mario, the daring rescuer of Princess Toadstool. The evil Wart, who holds her captive, has cast a magic spell on the Land of Dreams. But *your* power is greater.

Less familiar, but just as ominous, are nonelectronic games like *Phenomenon—The Game That Goes One Step Beyond.* Promising those who are twelve and older "The Extra Sensory Party," it offers to teach you *telepathy* ("the fun of transmitting images"), *clairvoyance* ("Is what you see what you get?"), *dermal vision* ("seeing" with your skin), and *psychometry* ("Can personal objects reveal your secret past?"). The game's promotion reads:

> *Everyone has psychic potential. Some call it hunch. Others call it intuition. It's a feeling the telephone is going to ring and sensing who is calling.* . . .
>
> Phenomenon . . . *gives you a chance to explore, unlock, and develop your psychic ability during a fun, fascinating game. What's more, you and your friends are doing it together.*

In a world that has lost its awe of God and its wariness of His enemy, why not try? Why not experiment with anything that offers secret knowledge, thrills, and power? Who worries about consequences in a New Age that denies sin, guilt and the sovereignty of God?

☐ Counterfeit values. When I was a child, I spanked my dolls when they "disobeyed." Whether we played "house" indoors, built tree houses in the forest, or dug ice caves outside in the five-foot snowpacks, we followed the rules that had become an accepted part of life. Our playtimes generally affirmed honesty, parental authority, and love.

The cartoons behind today's toys create a different atmosphere—where macho pride replaces gentleness, and cruel sarcasm supplants kindness; where unpunished aggression and violence imply the absence of true-to-life consequences. Here a child learns the specific actions and attitudes that define his posable toy.

Supermen call for superwomen, and toy shelves abound with slender beauties modeling physical perfection and flashy fashions. *Barbie* set the trend and others followed. Today's little girls learn the importance of having all of Barbie's fashion accessories: a styling center with makeup (the box shows a little girl hugging her makeup bag), an incredible wardrobe of designer clothes, a townhouse, furniture, a horse, an all-terrain vehicle and, of course, a boyfriend named Ken. If that isn't enough, she can borrow from Maxi—a Barbie clone—a sailboat, a windsurfer, a scooter, a hot tub.... Enough?

A gorgeous assortment of glittery princesses like *Lacy, Spacy,* and *Ultra Violet* compete for little girls' affection. Violet, a Cosmic Beauty Expert, comes with a complete line of Lacy Space fashions.

Less fantastic but just as flashy, *Today's Girls* know what counts. Kelly, "the most popular girl in school . . . has got her scene totally together from her outfit to her accessories. . . . It's like a party whenever [Katie] is around, with surprises up her sleeve (rock star posters, concert tickets, etc.). . . ." And Pepper is "always ready for a shopping spree with her truly outrageous outfit."

In spite of the feminist drive for sexual equality, girls' toys emphasize glamour, glitter, and seductive sensuality, while boys' toys encourage macho violence, ugly monsters, and supernatural power.

The New Age Dream World

In the hands of gullible preschoolers, toy supermen and powerwomen affirm the lie that man can control the "good" forces of the universe and conquer the evil forces. The friendly Care Bears remind them that with loving vibes they can create a world of peace and love.

Adults around the world believe that today. So does He-

Man, the Master of the Universe. Adversaries to peace in Eternia employ all forms of demonic power—witchcraft, magic, sorcery, and necromancy—to undermine his authority. But wise, handsome He-Man and strong, beautiful She-Rah always triumph. Wouldn't our leader-hungry, evolution-minded earth love a He-Man?

Children flock to video, arcade, and role-playing games filled with supernatural images and demonic suggestions. Blind to the true nature of evil, they play the part of gods in fantasy worlds where dragon power, spell-casting, and sorcery become thrilling solutions to man's struggles.

Jeffrey, a freshman class representative to the student council, played on the high school junior varsity football team in rural Wamego, Kansas. "An average, everyday student," he showed no signs of despondency or other special problems—until the day, February 6, 1985, when he shot himself in the head. All the clues linked Jeffrey's death to *Dungeons and Dragons*. "He wanted to go to the fantasy world of elves and dwarves instead of the world of reality with conflict," said the coroner. "It led to his death. He had been obsessed with [the game]."[2]

"The National Coalition on Television Violence claims there have been as many as 109 deaths resulting from heavy involvement in the fantasy role-playing game of *Dungeons and Dragons*. . . . Eighty . . . were murders or suicides."[3] D & D players live in a fantasy world of mazes, monsters, and magic. Obsessed with the game, many go on to other occult activities.

An Ominous Fascination With the Hideous

Perhaps you remember the *Madballs*—grotesque bouncing heads with matching names like Wolf Breath, Swine Sucker, Screamin' Meenie. Their inventor, Ralph Shaffer, commented that his successful minispheres would "take the world of cute-ugly into a new direction."

That was in 1986, when ugly-ugly as well as the cute-ugly were turning the corner and pulling our culture with them. Grotesque, demonic-looking creatures with fiery eyes invaded toy stores—and stayed. Many were mutants—part animal and part human, or a mixture of various animals and monsters—and most could wield supernatural power.

They won incredible popularity. Children seem to want these ugly hybrid, mutant supernaturals on their wallpaper, curtains, lunchboxes, and T-shirts. They love to cuddle the little demons. One supernatural, *Dark Dragon*, has black wings and a huge tail with red scales along the sides. It has a lion's mouth, teeth, and claws. Its eyes are glowing red, and out of the center of its forehead shines a large, green third eye. Its chest opens to reveal a skull. Another, *Black Star*, rides on a green horse with huge batlike wings and a long blue, orange, and green dragon tail. Its eyes are glowing red and a long tongue dangles from its mouth.

In a lecture titled "The Rising Interest in the Supernatural," Larry McLain, coauthor of *The Early Earth*, compares today's grotesque toys to the gods of the ancients:

> These [creatures] that show up in archeology and what we would call mythology were not just figments of the imagination. They were literal physical demonic entities that appeared to civilizations of the past. These types of demigods or demonic beings were represented as part human and part animal in their characteristics like this bird-human of the Assyrians. [They can be] horse and human like centaurs. Or fish and human like the god Dagon of the Philistines . . . or part jaguar and part human. Notice that tongue hanging out over the chin—which is a universal symbol of demonic possession. . . . One of the most popular combinations is human and serpent. You can find them on the toy shelves. It's not surprising that pagan religions worshiped serpents and dragons, for the Bible tells us in Revelation 12 that the old serpent, the dragon, is Satan the devil.[4]

Nor should today's growing popularity of demonic symbols surprise us. The Bible prophesies that demonic activities will escalate before and during the reign of the Antichrist. Could the multiplication of demonic-looking, alien images be part of Satan's plan to prepare us for these awful future events? Even for an invasion of demons?

Some New Agers have circulated an interesting theory

concerning the coming disappearance of millions of Christians: A fleet of UFO's and extraterrestrials will suddenly swoop down to earth to abduct all who resist mankind's spiritual evolution toward New Age global oneness.

Revelation 9:1-11 foresees a day when the Abyss (the bottomless pit where Satan will be cast for a thousand years) will open with a burst of smoke and release an army of powerful, deadly creatures onto the earth. They will look like a mixture of man, horse, and locust, with wings, "tails and stings like scorpions." Their commander will be Satan himself. Our God will allow it; for man's evil—as in the days of Noah—will call forth this judgment.

Though children are born with a natural fear of ugly, unusual creatures, this protection has been dulled by massive media exposure and training through toys. Children are being conditioned to embrace demonic manifestations, whether they come as intelligent rescuers from outer space or as evolved mutations from earth itself.

Our generation won't be shocked by the demonic invasion. They are actually anticipating that extraterrestrial intelligent beings, who look very different from us, will some day contact the earth and help us with ecological, monetary, and political problems. (Larry MacLain)

Why wouldn't they believe these lies? Today's belief in evolution leads them to trust that other forms of life must have evolved elsewhere. "After all," say humanists, "there is no God, but if He existed, He wouldn't have created the whole universe just for earthlings."

Maybe He would. Maybe God, who sent His own Son to die for us, would create a universe so vast that man's ego—which wants to explain every mystery without God's help—could not be satisfied. Maybe He did it to show us the immeasurable greatness of His sovereign, creative powers and the infinite width, length, height, and depth of His magnificent love. I believe He did.

CHAPTER TWELVE

What Can Parents Do About Distortions of Imagination?

Toys should reinforce, not contradict, the positive values we are trying to instill. (Phil Phillips, Turmoil In the Toybox)

When eight-year-old Joshua's parents found out what he wanted for Christmas, they felt put on the spot. Joshua had eyes only for the newest rage—*Nintendo*—along with its most popular game, *Super Mario Brothers II.* Anything else was "boring."

Joshua's folks had heard disturbing stories about *Nintendo* addiction—or whatever you call that intense focus that tolerates no interruption. So they didn't relish battling that obsession at bedtime—or any time. A rather pricey toy, *Nintendo* promised to zap a sizable hole in their budget, and the local stores had already sold out their allotment of *SMB II.*

Last year it was simple for Mom and Dad. Joshua just wanted more figures and accessories for the *Masters of the Universe.* The cost was tolerable, and they provided a year's worth of imaginative play. Of course, the gruesomeness of some of the figures caused them uneasiness.

Heidi's parents faced a similar dilemma. Their six-year-old daughter asked for Barbie's *Dream House*—fully furnished, of course—and a Maxie spa and patio furniture. "They fit together," she explained, "and everybody has them."

Barbie's long-time popularity fails to endear her to Heidi's concerned parents. They often wonder if the doll's curvy figure and flashy clothes might encourage values and sophistication inconsistent with their hopes for Heidi. What kinds of aspirations are built by these symbols of self-centered materialism?

If Barbie were the only messenger of hedonistic self-interest, a few more accessories would hardly matter. But pagan decadence beckons children everywhere. "Just throw off all restraints," it shouts, "and let human nature lead the way. Follow your feelings."

It's tough to teach restraint to children who are begging for gratification. Schools and the media have often declared parents the "bad guys." We feel the confusing values gap and flinch at the thought of playing censor once again. Yet we must. God has told us, the parents, to train our children to follow His way, and we can't turn back now. Also, He promises to enable us. Fortified with truth, let's make sure our children have toys that enhance their progress toward God's kind of maturity.

Step One: Develop a Sensitivity to Evil

A young mother driving a carload of children—including two from her church—posed this question: "Who is the Master of the universe?" "He-Man!" shouted a chorus of voices. The mother grieved as the youngsters praised their idol. Her heart sank further when one boy pulled an ugly figure from his pocket and waved it in the air. "And this is Hordak," he shouted. "He's bad! He fights He-Man!"

Current delight in false gods and demonic creatures may have begun with winsome magicians such as Papa Smurf and Rainbow Brite. As people welcomed these nonthreatening harbingers of occult forces, they unknowingly opened the door to the grotesque and disturbing realms of the dark occult.

At first we parents closed our eyes to this trend—we didn't want to overreact. Even within the church community, talk about Satan and his dark realm was often regarded as too negative or heavyhanded. Since we failed to resist, we gradually adapted and then accepted these practices. Now it's time to retrench, take our positions, and fight to regain our discernment and freedom. How do we do this?

☐ Continue to read and apply Scriptures.

☐ Share your own observations. Spark awareness in a young child with comments such as, "That monster looks gross!" or "That creature reminds me of a snake," along with "Did you know that in the Bible, serpents always represent Satan and evil?"

☐ To express your feelings to a young child, comment, "Who would want that evil-looking figure? I don't even like to look at him. Let's find something that makes us feel happy inside."

In the many ways we express our pleasure and displeasure, our disappointments and enthusiasms, our concern and criticism, our approval and disapproval, we pass on a set of values that usually runs longer and stronger than most outside messages. (Joanne Oppenheim in *Buy Me! Buy Me!*)

☐ Model wise decision-making. Tell your child why you wouldn't want to buy certain things.

☐ When a child wants something questionable, ask questions that are prayerfully adapted to your child's age, such as:

–What does the toy (or game) teach you (about power, about magic, about God, about yourself)? Discuss both obvious and subtle messages.

–Have you seen movies, cartoons, or comic books that made this toy (game) part of a story? What did the story tell you about it? Does the toy (game) remind you of someone who uses magic or supernatural power? Did someone pretend to be God?

–What does it teach about violence or immorality and their consequences?

–Does the toy (game) have any symbols or characteristics that associate it with either the light or dark side of New Age occultism?

Whatever is lovely, gracious, and good originates with

SYMBOLS—WHAT DO THEY TELL US?

Counterfeit	Genuine
Rainbow: Healing vibrations, a bridge to higher consciousness, the state of perfection, oneness with God.	God gave rainbows as a sign of His eternal covenant with man.
Pentagram: Five-pointed star. Pointing up, it represents light, life, and education. Pointing down, it represents evil, witchcraft, and black magic.	God put stars in the skies and uses them to illustrate the magnitude of His marvelous creation.
The Sun: The cosmic force, the all-seeing mind of the universe, the center of being.	God's provision for light, heat, and energy. One day we won't need it, for God's glory will illumine His heaven. (Revelation 22:5)
Sword: Used in satanic rituals to invoke the presence of Satan. A key symbol on Tarot cards.	The "Sword of the Spirit" is the Word of God. Take it, know it, wield it! (Ephesians 6:10-17)
Dragons or Serpents: Often charming, shrewd power-figures. Usually evil.	Biblical usage always refers to Satan or his shrewdness.
A Goat's Head: an integral part of satanic worship.	Scapegoat (Numbers 7:16) Separate sheep from goats. (Matthew 25:32)
Peace Symbol: distorted, upside-down cross, one of the many ways Satan mocks and misuses the cross.	The true cross—peace with God and victory over sin through Christ's atoning death.

God. Satan cannot produce anything new. All he can offer is counterfeits or clever distortions of God's gifts.

Rather than letting fear of the counterfeit turn you away from the genuine, be sure you know the difference. For example, while star pentagrams have become popular occult symbols—they also shine innocently from the blue field on our American flag. Pray for discernment to reject what is counterfeit, but thankfully to receive the good.

Step Two: Encourage Your Child To Choose the Good

Develop a mind-set that seeks the best, not just the "OK." You have identified and rejected the bad toys. But the rest are not necessarily good. Discuss these questions to help your child learn to choose the best. Phrase the questions according to your child's age level.

☐ Does it present a true picture of life? In a time when even adults base their lives on counterfeit dreams and false illusions, our children need to learn to tell what is real.

☐ How long would the interest last? Fad toys are fun for the moment, but they whet the appetite for every "in" thing, so that decision-making centers on the question, "What will make me *feel* happy right *now?*" Determine not to buy that lie. Unfortunately, many quality toy companies, like Creative Playthings, have been bought up or squeezed out by giants who can pay the high price for television promotion. The range of major toy lines is narrowing to those that look glamorous on the screen.[1]

☐ Will this toy be used for playing alone or with others? A child needs a balance of solitary and social play. Good toys will help him interact both with his imaginary world and with the real world, harmonizing the two. That may require some interaction with you. Perhaps you could agree together to find toys that will help you, the parent, participate in your young child's imaginary world.

☐ Can you shift the toy from its pre-set play pattern and use it for good? One mother found a way to remove Barbie from her glamorous me-centered world to one that fosters kindness and wholesome family life:

We sought to encourage a new emphasis in our daughter's Barbie play. . . . She had always played family games with her teenage dolls. In fact, Ken and Barbie were once "married" during a candlelight service, with her pastor/father officiating. We had transformed a cardboard box into a family home. Sarah Jane was open to extending the family, so we added a smaller doll with a little-girl face and figure. The family now included a child.[2]

☐ Does it build godly character? Many toys, hobbies, and games do. Review the biblical principles suggested for evaluating movies and television programs.

Step Three: Train Your Child To Follow God, Not Peers

We want our children to feel good about themselves, be liked by their peers, and not miss out on the fun. But as we realize what their friends choose, we wonder how our children will respond to the peer pressure. How can we prepare them to make wise choices?

☐ Counter their pressure. Children naturally compare us to the parents of peers, challenging us to match their "generosity." That hurts, since we want them to feel our love for them. We see what they don't realize: that getting the toys they want will not make them feel secure in our love. Instead, it increases their craving and builds discontent. Also, it teaches them to equate love with material things. If your child is old enough, explain this process to him.

☐ Teach them to be individuals, not just members of the status quo. The New Age tells children that "all are one." The truth is that God made each person unique. Wisdom resists false justifications like, "Everybody has one!" (Discuss Deuteronomy 7:6 and 2 Corinthians 6:14-18).

☐ Discuss whether "showing off" might be their motive for wanting a toy. Feeding that feeling produces bondage and increased insecurity.

Children as well as adults crave superior luxury items and toy manufacturers are quick to comply.

☐ Be a pacesetter. Have an abundant supply of ideas and tools to help your child and his friends use their imaginations and develop their own play: dress-up clothes (thrift stores are a good resource), fabrics for making puppets, scrap wood for outdoor structures, a refrigerator carton for making a playhouse, etc.

☐ Look to the Bible for guidelines and authority. God understands our desires to follow the crowd; He feels our struggle to be "in" the world but not "of" it (John 17:16-18). According to age readiness, review Romans 12:1-2 together and then discuss 3 John 11 and Jude 18-20.

☐ Self-denial seems out of place in a nation consumed with self-indulgence and self-fulfillment. But God commanded it and Jesus demonstrated it. Dare we refuse to acknowledge it? According to the age of your child, discuss Jesus' words in Matthew 16:24 and then allow the Holy Spirit to direct your application.

Don't get me wrong. Far more than earthly parents, God wants His children to be happy and have a good time. But He doesn't want cream puffs to satisfy our hunger and turn us away from the meat of truth. Self-discipline produces the kind of maturity that brings genuine happiness forever, not merely a pleasant moment today.

Our Heavenly Father, who models parenting better than any of us, doesn't major on the superficial. He knows better than to give us all the things we want. For just as most children will choose pop over milk, and chips over carrots, so we as adults often choose that which cannot satisfy. God does not want empty vanities, as He calls them, to mold our appetites, satisfy our hunger, and replace the very best.

> *Oh, the depth of the riches of the wisdom and knowledge of God! How unsearchable are His judgments, and His paths beyond tracing out!*
>
> *Who has known the mind of the Lord? Or who has been His counselor? Who has ever given to God, that God should repay him?*
>
> *For from Him and through Him and to Him are all things. To Him be the glory forever! (Romans 11:33-36)*

CHAPTER THIRTEEN
Books and Magazines and Offensive Titillation

Literature, perhaps more than any other kind of expression, has faithfully chronicled the New Age. A host of fiction and nonfiction work, many already ascribed "classic" status, present the gospel of the twentieth century to anyone who can read—or knows someone who can. (Alice and Stephen Lawhead in Pilgrim's Guide *to the New Age)*

While relatives and friends cheered their favorite team, two girls huddled in the lower left corner of the stands, oblivious to the thrills of a championship Little League game. They sat bent over a magazine. Only occasionally did they break their silent concentration to point out something special on a page, to giggle, or to share a look of surprise.

Toward the end of the game, the two young teens finally closed the magazine and exposed the title: *Sassy.* Curious about its power to hold their attention, I bought a copy at the local supermarket the next day.

It opened my eyes to a new teen culture. (Or, is the new teen culture being formed by *Sassy* and other pacesetters?) In addition to gorgeous faces and bodies matched with corresponding beauty tips, it showed how to stay physically fit and "get the coolest look going." After putting on a pair of black Lycra biking shorts and a T-shirt sporting a picture of a glaring skull, "slap some skate stickers, like metallic skulls and peace signs, on everything in sight. Anything else you can find with crossbones, '60s' symbols and gore galore (like severed hands and heads) will do it too. . . . Now pick up the latest issue of *Thrasher* magazine, start saying words like 'tear, thrash and rip.' "[1]

Through compassionate interviews, *Sassy* brought the reader into the hearts of lesbian and gay couples. It encouraged its reader to use a cervical cap, know the best rock groups, and see the right movies. For example, avoid the low-rated (or near bomb) *Casual Sex*. "After all, what's so funny about watching a couple of L.A. chicks doing what *every average sexually active* person on Earth is doing?"[2]

One page brought the reader up to date on what was "sassy" these days—groovy words like *groovox*; and what was not—stone-washed denims. Under the column, "Comic Books Are Your Friends," it gave a list of "which comic books are hippest: *The Uncanny X-Men*, *Batman: The Killing Joke*, *Lone Wolf and Club*, *ElfQuest*, and *Tales of the Teenage Mutant Ninja Turtles.*[3]

I decided that if this is what the girls are reading, I'd better check it out. So I stopped by the local comic book store and read off the list to the salesman. He pointed to *his* display of the latest hits. My list matched his. Since he had sold the last *Batman: The Killing Joke*, he suggested I substitute with *The Punisher*, and *Mai, the Psychic Girl*—two more top sellers. Because I was beginning to feel uncomfortable in his shop, I quickly bought them all.

"How old are the kids who buy these," I asked before hurrying out.

"Every age," he answered. "From little kids to adults."

"How can kids afford it?"

"No problem," he smiled. "They've got bucks!"

When I arrived home and began to skim through these contemporary treasures, I could hardly believe what I saw. Young children read this? Pornography, cruelty, sadism, violence, and occultism leaped out from the pages. In less than five minutes I had skimmed through all I could take.

Selfism, Sex, and Violence

The word *sassy* describes an attitude modeled in today's movies, peer groups, and classrooms as well: "given to back talk, impertinent, physically vigorous, distinctively smart or stylish."[4] It matches the selfism rampant today: I choose my own way, create my own reality; I am essentially perfect and divinely powerful; I am my own god!

Have you noticed how consistently this arrogant attitude comes through popular comic strips? Lazy, cynical *Garfield*, the macabre humor of *Far Side*, and the delightful, incorrigible *Calvin and Hobbes* demonstrate the same deception: success and popularity come by arrogant self-confidence, macho self-sufficiency, manipulative control, and a sarcastic kind of put-down that masquerades as humor.

The young adult section of our local library—"for twelve-year-olds to high school seniors," says our librarian—spreads a more subtle form of the "sassy" attitude. Tempting adult-sized novels make humanist/New Age values seem normal, fun, and beautiful.

Judy Blume, "godmother of upscale adolescent realism,"[5] writes captivating novels for preteens and adolescent girls. While her books seek to guide children through some of the most confusing years of their lives, they also accomplish what humanists demand and teenagers desire: the separation of sexual cravings and expressions from all social or spiritual restraints. They answer questions, delight the imagination, and help teenagers overcome fears, "old-fashioned misconceptions," and guilt.

Kids have a right to read about decent kids who are involved in sexual relationships and nothing bad happens. Sex without punishment is very important. (Judy Blume)

Blume's *Forever*, "the volume most requested by teens in the New York Public Library," tells about a young girl's first experiences with sexual intimacy. A heartwarming and persuasive story, it gives young readers an encouraging how-to manual for intercourse, birth control, and handling concerned parents: "Don't tell them, for it is 'hard for parents to accept the facts.' "[6]

Equally hard for parents to accept are the facts behind our children's popular role models. Beckoning from a rack in the children's library, *Duran-Duran* by Toby Goldstein tells about the "cute" rock group that pioneered pornographic music videos. Leaving out the sordid details of their seductive songs and films, the book presents an enticing commercial for Duran-Duran's demoralizing products.

The violence and vulgarity in *The Chocolate Wars* by Robert Cormier do not prevent it from being required reading for many eighth-graders. Concerning its author, a book editor for *San Jose Mercury News* comments: "Nobody who's fifteen wants a kiddie book, and Cormier doesn't write 'em. His thrillers come with adult-sized portions of sex, disillusionment, intrigue, and conflict. In *Fade*, he crosses *The Invisible Man, The Bad Seed*, and the collected works of Stephen King."[7]

Promoting New Age Beliefs and Practices

A selection of "bedtime fantasies to build self-esteem" fills a pretty little book by Michael Pappas titled, *Sweet Dreams for Little Ones*. One of them reads: "Your name is ____ Strong. You have special powers. . . . You are very strong and can lift anything that you want to, no matter how big or heavy it is. . . . You use your power only to help people."[8]

While this may sound appealing, like many of the beautiful children's books available today, it teaches Guided Imagery—but not by God's Spirit; Visualization—but not based on truth; Supernatural Power—but not God's.

Remember, the best counterfeit is the most dangerous deception. And it may not be new. If you didn't read *The Secret Garden* as a child, you could hardly miss it today. Prominently displayed in bookstores, it has experienced an amazing revival because it fits the basic New Age tenets.

When I first read it, I didn't notice that Francis Hodgson Burnett had written a persuasive argument for pantheism. Without preaching, she identifies her god: a gentle, healing force that permeates all of nature. She calls it Magic.

Typical of most manifestations of "the beautiful side of

It is true that what we think influences how we act. But [The Secret Garden] is saying more than that. It is saying that ideas actually make things happen. What we think creates reality. [This] is akin to the occult view that the material world is an emanation of mental and spiritual reality—and therefore if we change the mental world, we can create a new material reality.[9]

evil," this magic takes on divine characteristics and accomplishes marvelous feats—just like God. Hear it from the children's mouths. Notice how their beloved Magic exhibits all the characteristics of a New Age god.

☐ God is in everything (pantheism). "Everything is made out of Magic," says invalid Colin, "leaves and trees, flowers and birds, badgers and foxes and squirrels and people. ...The Magic is in me....It is in everyone of us...."[10] India-born Mary and Dickon, who share a special oneness with plants and animals, agree. They taught him.

☐ God is an impersonal force. "If you keep calling it [the Magic] to come to you and help you, it will get to be part of you and it will stay and do things."[11]

☐ Man can control and harness this cosmic power through mental exercises, creating his own imagined reality. "Every morning and evening..." vows Colin, "I am going to say, 'Magic is in me! Magic is making me well!' "[12] Later the children sit cross-legged under a tree—"like sitting in sort of a temple"—as Colin chants affirmations about the Magic, ending with, "Magic! Magic! Come and help!"[13]

In the end, a strong, happy Colin testifies to the power of Magic—and to Satan's delight in focusing man's faith on a compliant substitute for God.

Loving the Occult

"What kinds of books do you like to read?" I asked a ten-year-old.

"Science fiction," she answered.

"What are some of your favorites?"

"The books by Zilpha Keatley Snyder. I just finished *The*

Headless Cupid." She told me the story.

"That sounds more like psychic fiction than science fiction. What do you think?"

"I guess so. But it's real adventuresome."

"How do you feel when you read stories like *The Headless Cupid?* Spooky and a little scared?"

"It's exciting and fun. I like it."

The children's library has other books by Snyder. "Fifth- and sixth-graders love them! affirmed the librarian. I checked out *The Witches of Worm*, a story about a demon-possessed kitten who gets a lonely little girl into all sorts of trouble. In the end, the heroine researches witchcraft, learns an occult version of exorcism, and apparently proves man's power to subdue the irrascible forces of evil.

Preschoolers also love the scary and magical. Beautiful picture books tell ugly stories about witchcraft, magic, and sorcery. A book for toddlers, *Little Witch's Magic Spells*, even comes with a toy witch.

Elementary children read books like *Bunnicula* by Deborah and James Howe—a tale about a little dracula bunny who mysteriously escapes his cage each night to scavenge in the kitchen. Mom and Dad just can't figure out why vegetables turn white and have fang marks in them.

Worn pages and wrinkled covers prove the popularity of library series like the *Dragontales* and *Endless Quest* books, where the reader is the hero. Both equip youngsters with every kind of occult power.

The latter is published by the producers of *Dungeons and Dragons*. In Rose Estes' *Dragon of Doom*, you conquer an evil magician with your magical ring, spells, mind-linking with your companions to strengthen the force, entering into trance states, clairvoyance, mental telepathy, and the wisdom of today's "values clarification." Confronting the dreaded Dragon of Doom, you offer this contemporary guideline which supposedly justifies any action: "[Destroy mankind] because *you choose to* and not because you have been ordered to do so. It must be your decision."[14]

Libraries and book stores offer an equally menacing menu to teenagers. Even sixth- and seventh-graders devour seductive medleys of science fiction, sex, occult, and psychic adventure—including the adult horrors of Stephen King. These fantasies draw their minds into a demonic dream world where psychic phenomena, sensual highs, and occult terrors become as familiar as roses and rainbows.

Painting a New World

The cruel power struggle of *The Chocolate Wars* illustrates the selfishness of human nature and the horrors of anarchy. Without some kind of strength to maintain peace and justice, the strong will oppress the weak—in schools, in communities, in cities, in nations, and around the world. History proves it. Yet man continues to reach for fragile bubbles, like the dream of a more perfect mankind who— apart from God—can stop competing and live in peace.

The Butter Battle Book by Dr. Seuss, a tragicomic globalist parable, implies that wars rise from trivial differences such as buttering bread on the wrong side—which is what the Zooks do! But the Yooks spread their bread "with the butter side up ... the right, honest way!"[15]

The silly war between the Yooks and Zooks escalates from slingshots to the Bitsy Big-Boy Boomeroo, a Seuss-sized atom bomb. Meanwhile the Right-Side-Up Girls sing an inspiring anthem: "Oh, be faithful! Believe in thy butter!"

The last page shows two representatives—Grandpas Yook and Zook—each ready to drop the deadly bomb over enemy territory. The final words seem designed to raise fear, but—like globalist programs in schools—offer only a biased, uninformed glimpse of an extremely complex and painful dilemma. "Grandpa," I shouted, "be careful! Oh Gee! Who's going to drop it? Will you ... ? Or will he ... ?"[16]

We all hate war. We want to live. But sometimes God calls us to stand firm in what we believe—even to the point of risking our lives. Of course, this kind of self-sacrifice is not an issue these days. Self-fulfillment is, and the world offers many tempting ways.

Older children feast on a fantastic assortment of futuristic dreams. While science fiction needs no scientific basis, it builds plausible visions of an evolving universe and an omnipotent mind—whether human, robotic, or alien. Some stories are witty and nonsensical like Douglas Adams' series on *The Hitchhiker's Guide to the Galaxy.* (You can even get a matching video game.) Others tell about global overpopulation, resettlements on other planets, time travel, fantastic humanoid robots who free man from the drudgery of work, mental, and spiritual transcendence, "probability patterns" that break every impossible barrier. . . . Often the fantastic illusions include distorted images of God— molded to fit the author's dream—along with selected Scriptures to add credibility.

If students can discern between fiction and fact, some of these books provide thought-provoking reading. But we should not let futuristic visions and unwarranted fears obscure God's view of the future. The Bible tells us that God is preparing a new world where His love and power will guarantee genuine peace. He invites everyone to come. The door—Jesus Christ Himself—stands open and waiting. As He watches, He weeps over those who turn to go their own way. For the tragedy is that while Jesus loves all people, most of them are distracted by counterfeit visions of present and future life, and few accept His invitation.

Meanwhile, God is training His people for eternity with Him. He equips us to follow truth in a world that hates His Word and writes its own gospel. Are your children prepared to recognize and resist the counterfeit?

I keep asking that the God of our Lord Jesus Christ, the glorious Father, may give you the Spirit of wisdom and revelation, so that you may know Him better. I pray also that the eyes of your heart may be enlightened in order that you may know the hope to which He has called you, the riches of His glorious inheritance in the saints, and His incomparably great power for us who believe. (Ephesians 1:17-19)

CHAPTER FOURTEEN
What Can Parents Do About Offensive Titillation?

When children from nine years of age upward are led to believe that [contemporary teen novels] reflect how most people live, then their conduct will certainly be influenced. . . . If more acceptable conduct is desired by society, then society must hold before young people more acceptable conduct. (Pro-Family Forum)

Literature that fails to thrill, titillate, or terrorize doesn't get far in today's secular marketplace. Shallow and provocative substitutes for good literature seduce rather than build noble character. Traditionally, the classroom has been a purveyor of character-building books. It still is, but what kind of values does it now build?

In the fall of 1988, my son's eighth-grade English teacher required her students to read Jay McInerney's *Bright Lights, Big City*. The setting: a nightclub for singles, in the wee hours of the night. The hero: "You."

You spot a girl at the edge of the dance floor who looks like your last chance for earthly salvation. . . . There she is in her pegged pants, a kind of doo-wop retro ponytail pulled off to the side, as eligible a candidate as you are likely to find this late into the game. The sexual equivalent of fast food.

She shrugs and nods when you ask her to dance. You like the way she moves, the oiled ellipses of her hips and shoulders. After the second song, she says she's tired. She's at the point of bolting when you ask her if she needs a little pick-me-up.

"You've got some blow?" she says.

"Is Stevie Wonder blind?" you say.

> *She takes your arm and leads you into the Ladies'. A couple*
> *of spoons and she seems to like you just fine, and you are feel-*
> *ing very likable yourself. A couple more. This woman is all*
> *nose.*
> *"I love drugs," she says, as you march toward the bar.*
> *"It's something we have in common," you say.*
> *"Have you ever noticed how all the good words start with D?"*
> *" . . . You know. Drugs. Delight. Decadence."*
> *"Debauchery," you say, catching the tune now.*
> *"Dexedrine."*
> *"Delinquent."[1]*

A discussion with my son's teacher resulted in a change
in reading assignments. Yet it takes more than an occasional win to slow society's downward drift. In *Amusing
Ourselves to Death,* Neil Postman compares the chilling
prophecies of two authors, Orwell and Aldous Huxley:

> *Orwell feared that the truth would be concealed from us. Huxley*
> *feared the truth would be drowned in a sea of irrelevance.*
> *Orwell feared we would become a captive culture. Huxley*
> *feared we would become a trivial culture, preoccupied with*
> *some equivalent of the feelies, the orgy porgy, and the centrifu-*
> *gal bumblepuppy. . . . In* 1984 *. . . people are controlled by in-*
> *flicting pain. In* Brave New World, *they are controlled by inflict-*
> *ing pleasure. In short, Orwell feared that what we hate will*
> *ruin us. Huxley feared that what we love will ruin us.[2]*

Postman suggests that Huxley, not Orwell, was right. I
believe that if Huxley was right, Orwell's reality will follow.
New Age optimists, who believe man's inherent goodness
will lead him on an upward journey to spiritual perfection,
have, in Huxley's words, "failed to take into account man's
almost infinite appetite for distractions."

America still reads, but popular books aim to entertain,
not inform. Thrills sell. Facts don't. A charismatic world
leader needs no military weapons, only promises, to take
control over a hedonistic and nonthinking people.

I am not a pessimist. Our King has won the war, fill us
with Himself, and promised us a glorious future. We don't
need to fear anything—other than turning our backs on

God. And if we awaken to the current challenge, we can make a difference in the world.

Step One: Personal Preparation

Are children being taught to read discerningly, or do they accept whatever is in print simply because it *is* in print?

□ Pray as a family for discernment and wisdom. Don't let fear of offensive literature stop your family from feasting on wonderful books.

□ Commit yourself to a deeper knowing of the Living Word. Continue a daily Bible study program together. If children know truth, they will spot the lies.

□ Enjoy books together that demonstrate God's values. Read-aloud times build in most children a deep love for reading, while they also enable you to direct your children's taste for enriching books. "While the average first-grade student reads from a primer with only 350 words, his *listening* vocabulary approaches 10,000 words, according to the Council for Basic Education."[3]

When you read aloud to your children, they learn to associate good books with cozy times. C.S. Lewis' Narnia books make wonderful family reading. Not only did we read them aloud together, our older sons reread them in high school, and Todd, our oldest, read them aloud again with his college roommate.

When the father and mother tell the stories, they can stop and explain the stories, tell them over and over, remold them, shape them for the child. (Bruno Bettelheim)

Step Two: Recognize Deception in Magazines

□ Discuss magazine displays with your child, if and when appropriate. Look at titles together and point out what is counterfeit. In addition to a broad selection of questionable teen magazines, I see the *Yoga Journal, East West, Magical Blend, Shaman's Drum, UFO, Hinduism Today,* and *Meditation.* If you haven't seen them yet, you will.

☐ Realize that magazines have changed. The January 1989 issue of *Seventeen* featured three main articles:

–"Spa Splurge"—"At last . . . your folks have disappeared, and the house is yours!"

–"Bad Boys—Why we love them so"—"A cute . . . good boy who has the same amount of experience you do . . . simply may not make you feel sexy and grown-up enough."

–"Are you ready for sex?"—"Until you have . . . a birth control method . . . [and know your boyfriend's sexual history] you are not ready."[4]

Across from the index page you see a young girl seductively posed in black stockings, black miniskirt, black leather jacket pulled open to reveal a chest bare except for a black metal lattice bra. Caption: "Some people are really into metal. They insist on it—even in unusual places . . . Swatch [the watch] gives you more than the time of day."

Step Three: Be Alert to Deception in Books

☐ A crossless version of Christianity fits the New Age lie that all can be one—with or without Jesus. It denies man's need for redemption and, in effect, makes man his own savior. "For the message of the Cross is foolishness to those who are perishing, but to us who are being saved it is the power of God" (1 Corinthians 1:18).

☐ Examine gift books for children. Discuss your observations with your child. Some of Audrey and Don Wood's attractive books are filled with enticing New Age magic. Other picture books, like *The Witches Handbook* by Malcolm Bird, treat witchcraft as a game for all to enjoy.

☐ Check contemporary children's poetry. While some poems are superb, others are grotesque and macabre.

☐ Check fantasy gamebooks. They make *you* the hero—but what beliefs do *you* follow? What mental pictures will your imagination create? As you make decisions appropriate to the story, will occult forces become part of your thinking? Some titles will warn you—like *Seas of Blood* and *Castle Death*—but many others sound innocuous.

☐ Be alert to what peers read. Discuss their influence with your child. During the winter of 1989, many of David's eighth-grade peers read *Cycle of the Werewolf* by Stephen King, master of occult horror.

☐ A new kind of joke book has captivated readers. The object of the humor may be sex, marriage, parents, or God. Some of the illustrations may be pornographic. While we desperately need a sense of humor, we don't need to laugh at corruption and delight in immorality. God wants us to love, accept, and forgive each other. But He also tells us to discipline and control our own human nature. Discuss these Scriptures with your child: Leviticus 11:44, 20:26; and Matthew 5:6, 8. Review Romans 12:1-2, 9, and 13:14.

Step Four: Check Your Library

☐ Befriend your local librarian. Learn your library's guidelines and limitations. Know its definition of adult literature and whether or not children can check it out.

Many decision-makers seem to deny essential differences that separate childhood from adulthood. Children have neither the knowledge, wisdom, or experience to make adult decisions and carry adult responsibility. Adult movies, television, and books feed children adult-sized mental stimulants that they are unprepared to handle.

The American Library Association's "Bill of Rights" states that, regardless of age, *all* persons have unlimited access to *all* library material. . . . In principle this eliminates any distinction between juvenile and adult sections. . . . Children have access to *all books!* Who gave the American Library Association the right to make this important decision? (Pro Family Forum)[5]

☐ Scan the books promoted in special displays for children and for young adults (teenagers). Do they promote anti-Christian religions or low values? Do biographies promote social philosophies that oppose Christianity? Are they balanced with other views? If not, our libraries become— like the media—a political force with incredible power to influence children according to their own bias.

☐ Discuss your concerns with the librarian. Observe the guidelines in Chapter 2. Suggest solutions. While your local librarians may share your values, the American Library Association denies the need to shield children from certain kinds of adult literature and illustrations.

Step Five: Join in the Battle for Truth

☐ Continue to pray with other Christian families for God's wisdom and direction.

☐ Write advertisers in offensive magazines. Under Dr. Dobson's leadership, a flood of parental protest against *Sassy's* style caused some of its major advertisers to withdraw. The consequent financial pressure seems to have made *Sassy* more responsible in its coverage.

☐ Keep an up-to-date church library and encourage other families to support and use it.

☐ Let God encourage you with biblical passages that promise victory to those who trust and follow Him. See Psalm 25:1, 4-5; Exodus 14:13-14; Deuteronomy 1:30; 20:1, 4.

SUGGESTED READING

The Read-Aloud Handbook by Jim Trelease
Honey for a Child's Heart by Gladys Hunt

CHAPTER FIFTEEN
Music and Pagan Sentiments

For primitive man music is not merely recreation or a form of self-expression but is an integral part of the world in which he lives. . . . Through music he finds a link with the supernatural. (Encyclopedia Britannica)

The one thing I got from Hitler was the idea of the Nazi youth. . . . The youth of today are the leaders of tomorrow. They're young, they can be brain-washed and programmed. (Nikki Sixx of the rock band Motley Crüe)[1]

Adventures into the world of Zen, free sex, and mind-expanding drugs during the '60s paved capricious paths to "higher" consciousness. The long hair of those years was merely a sign of broken boundaries, rebellion against authority, and experimental ways to live—and die.

Music nurtured this liberation. It summoned, taught, inspired, and unified the seekers. Those who sang the same words felt the same rhythms and caught the same visions.

Like New Age spirituality, the music of the New Age has developed through syncretism—a blending of contemporary dreams, ancient paganism, Eastern religions, and modern technology. The album jacket copy for Windham Hill's *Pioneers of the New Age* summarizes the thrill of discovery:

It was like a gardener's experiment in cross-pollination gone wild. Each different type of music fertilizing the other, producing a stunning hybrid flowering. John Coltrane mixed jazz with Eastern music. Bob Dylan mixed folk music with beat poetry and

electric guitars. Jimi Hendrix and The Beatles [added] elec-
tronics and multitracking. . . .

Two distinct forms of music have emerged. One, the
ambient sounds labeled "New Age Music," flows from a
growing fascination with Eastern meditative religions. Its
soothing, sometimes monotonous tones relax and often delight. Appealing to man's spiritual yearning for inner peace
and harmony with nature, it is *usually* harmless unless
accompanied by New Age visualizations. However, the
number of tapes composed to induce trance states is soaring.

The other kind—loud, physical rock—unashamedly
vaunts counterfeit or occult values, images, rhythms, and
verbal expressions. It has captured the hearts and minds of
children around the world.

On the surface, these two types of music seem as opposite as what they proclaim: inner peace or sensual violence. But they aim in the same direction: union with the
angel of light, the god of forces, who wants to immunize
children against truth and persuade them to worship idols.

You hypnotize people [with music] to where they go right back to
their natural state, which is pure positive . . . and when you get
people at that weakest point, you can preach into the subconscious
what we want to say. (Jimi Hendrix)[2]

Ancient Forms of New Age Music

The New Age includes the dark as well as the beautiful side
of evil. The mind behind the enticing masks hates God and
everything He represents. Thus New Age music includes
not merely the smooth, hypnotic strains that flow from
electric synthesizers, but the whole range of music that
lauds New Age enticements—and suggests the use of meditation, magic, and drugs to reach them.

Man's attempts to transcend the boundaries of the physical world through music weaves through the history of mankind. While God encouraged His people to worship and enter His presence through songs of praise, Satan—as he always does with God's best gifts—provided a counterfeit. Thus pagan societies used music to connect them with other gods. Nevill Drury, who promotes New Age meditation and visualization in his manual, *Music for Inner Space*, points to ancient cultures as models for today.

> *In societies where magic and myth define and influence everyday existence, man aspires to be like the gods and to imitate them, thereby acquiring mastery of nature.... In both primitive societies and ancient cultures, magical incantations and songs are a source of power.*[3]

In India, the ancient Hindu *ragas* stimulated the imagination. Drury explains that the drone component—"the unchanging basic note or pitch"—sustains the music and "meditatively makes each musical performance an 'inner journey.' One literally travels with the music, lured into new areas of consciousness...."[4]

Repetitive rhythms and mantric musical patterns are used universally to induce trance states. However, we have a choice within the altered state of allowing ourselves to surrender to the music and be "possessed" by its intoxicating rhythms or "ride" the music or drumbeat on our journey to the inner world. (Nevill Drury)

In primitive Africa and South America, the witch doctor functioned as a mediator between the tribe and demonic spirits. The sacred drum—credited with magical powers—together with hallucinatory drugs (sorcery) induced trances which transported him into the spirit world. There he received guidance.

Obo Addy, a drummer and singer from Ghana said, "My father was a medicine man. He told the future and healed the sick. Music invoked the spirits my father possessed."[5]

The ceremony often involved the whole tribe. Intoxicated by the drum's beat, the dancers would finally surrender to the persuasive rhythms and enter a state of trance. A description of the Macumba (Brazil) spiritists' trance dance ends with this observation: "If I was looking for a mindless joy it was here, in a dance with the brain turned off and the body taking its orders straight from the drum."[6]

Musicologists Manfred Clynes and Janice Walker explained that "the central nervous system transforms a musical rhythm into a movement pattern." This "rhythmic experience of sound largely is not under control—we are *driven* by it."[7] Nevill Drury explains:

> *The rhythms which induce trance states are repetitive, energetic, and often loud and overwhelming. They lead the dancer away from the familiar setting of the everyday world into a disorienting atmosphere pulsing with vibrant rhythms, which usually builds to a climax. In voodoo it is at this point that the* loa *gods possess and "ride" their subjects in trance like horses, while in Africa the dancers imitate the movements and footsteps of the possessing spirits.*[8]

The Intoxicating Message of Rock

Hard rock and heavy metal have soared to stardom, even among children. Heavy metal "differs from other forms of rock by its bombastic chords, screaming lead guitars, throat-wrenching vocals, and a demolition derby approach to drumming."[9] Dave Hart, a research analyst for Menconi Ministries, identifies three kinds of metal music.

☐ Party metal, the most popular style, emphasizes sex, drugs, partying, and living for today with no thought for tomorrow. "It's the stuff getting on the charts: Bon Jovi, Motley Crüe, Def Leppard," explains Hart. "There is very little overt occultism."[10]

It does, however, teach Satan's favorite messages: *Follow your feelings* and *Live to lust.* Mere explicit sex no longer shocks enough, so party metal has stooped to the level of kinky, cruel, and violent sex—"porn rock"—such as Judas Priest's song about oral sex at gunpoint.

□ Thrash metal joins punk music and heavy metal in a perverted focus on violence and death. " 'Eighty-six ways to die' is the theme of half of these albums,"[11] explains Hart. The album jackets flaunt hateful messages such as Megadeth's *Killing Is My Business—and Business Is Good*. Metallica's "Kill 'Em All," and Anthrax's "Spreading the Disease."

At concerts, "metalheads" or fans "shake their heads and hair vigorously to the beat. Many reel and career into each other in a wild style of dancing called 'moshing'—the punkers call it 'slam dancing.' Pity those who collapse under the feet of the feverish throng."[12]

Overexposure to violent images is desensitizing us to violence. Because it now takes more and more violence to make us feel shock and revulsion, media violence has to become more and more graphic to be profitable. We are addicted—and we're about to overdose. (Tipper Gore in *Raising PG Kids in an X-Rated Society*)

□ Black metal is satanic. The album jackets display grotesque pictures smattered with skulls, chains, blood, demons, goat heads in pentagrams, and a mockery of crosses. The titles proclaim the power of supernatural evil: Destruction's *Bestial Invasion*, Slayer's *Hell Awaits*, Venom's *From Hell to the Unknown*, and Iron Maiden's "Number of the Beast" from the album *Live After Death*.

Whether the musicians personally practice satanism or merely play at it for its shock value matters little to the children who absorb the messages. No doubt, the image of a vampirish Ozzy Osbourne drooling blood and singing about an "X-rated demon that lives in my head"[13] has inspired occult fascination in the hearts of his young worshipers who had moved beyond fear. Surely Venom's ritual images in the song, "Sacrifice" has fueled that curiosity:

"Sacrifice to Lucifer . . . /Bring the chalice/Raise the knife/
Welcome to my sacrifice. . . . "[14]

Given full freedom to indulge natural desires, many
youngsters learn to crave the most shocking, lewd and bru-
tal entertainment available.

When Darkness Rules

One of Webster's definitions for the word *muse*, the root of
music, is "the personification of a guiding genius or principal source of inspiration."

Man has two main sources of inspiration outside of himself: God and Satan. While both communicate their thoughts
to willing listeners, the latter is an aggressive liar who desires
to enflame rebellion against God. (See 1 Chronicles 21:1;
John 3:2, 27; Acts 5:3; 13:10; Ephesians 2:2-5.)

Many popular singers have acknowledged their links to a
supernatural source of inspiration other than God. For example, Joni Mitchel admitted being ruled by "a male muse
named Art" who opened to her "the shrine of creativity."[15]
Angus Young of AC/DC confessed, "Someone else is steer-
ing me. I'm just along for the ride. I become possessed
when I'm on stage."[16]

The fact that most rock singers look to themselves,
drugs, or alcohol for inspiration, not consciously to Satan
or spirit guides, fits the deceiver's plan perfectly. He is a
master at using untamed desires for his purposes.

God tells us not to give up on those who are caught in
deception. Instead He encourages us to speak the truth in
love so that "they will come to their senses and escape
from the trap of the devil, who has taken them captive to
do his will" (2 Timothy 2:26).

What Do Children Learn?

"Children spend an estimated four to six hours a day with
music. They get up to it, get dressed to it, do their homework to it, and fall asleep to it. That adds up to 11,000

hours of listening to music between the seventh and twelfth grades alone."[17]

Do children really listen to the words? Former disc jockey and rock musician Bob DeMoss travels throughout the United States speaking to parents, teachers, and kids. He tests grade-school students to prove that children learn the lyrics and often understand the adult message. Asked a question about the title of the Samantha Fox song, "Touch Me, (I Want Your ____)," eighty percent of the fourth-graders filled in the missing word "Body." Obvious familiarity enabled them to sing the words to George Michael's seductive "I Want Your Sex."[18]

Dr. Joseph Stuessy, professor of music theory at the University of Texas at San Antonio, contends: "There is a new element in the music, a meanness of spirit—outright hatred—that was not present in the early days of rock."[19] People are more likely to remember a musical message than words spoken alone. When you add the fact that repetition internalizes the message, the sum spells DANGER.

Most hard rock and heavy metal bands—whether through records, MTV, or concerts—drum the following anti-Christian messages into children's minds.

☐ Spurn Jesus Christ. Album jackets expose an incredible hatred of Christ. Replete with crosses of every kind— bloodied and broken, moss-covered, upside-down, even right-side-up but in an occult setting—they mock the symbol of Christ's victory. Metal Church's album, *Blessings in Disguise*, twists Christianity with song titles such as "Fake Healer" and "Rest in Pieces."

Venom spills out its rage on the cover of *Welcome to Hell:* "We're possessed by all that's evil. The death of your God we demand. . . ."[20]

Craig Chaquico of Jefferson Starship proclaims an alternative religion: "Rock concerts are the churches of today. Music puts them on a spiritual plane. All music is god."[21] "It's bad to be good," proclaims Poison,[22] illustrating the reversal so typical of satanic ideology.

In her video, *Like a Virgin*, Madonna makes herself the object of worship. Dressed in a lacy slip and a cross, the sex goddess writhes seductively in a mystical church setting resplendent with candles and crosses. Like an ancient cult prostitute, she blends sexual lust with spiritual worship—an occult formula that has proven its magnetism.

□ Sexual promiscuity, perversion, and violence. The children who listened to Prince's songs while doing their homework heard lyrics such as these from the album, *Dirty Mind:* "My sister never made love/To anyone else but me . . . /Incest is everything it's said to be."[23]

Megapopular Guns N' Roses rose to the top with its debut album, *Appetite for Destruction*, which sold over seven million copies. This band plays for "the kids"—and the kids love them. Ask any non-Christian nine- or ten-year-old. Then consider the impact of songs like "Anything Goes" on a child's mind: "Panties 'round your knees/With your ass in debris. . . ." The next lines present a graphic image of intercourse, then the song finishes with a hint of sadomasochism: "Tied up, tied down/Up against the wall/Be my rubbermade baby/And we can do it all."[24]

The original album cover for *Appetite For Destruction* showed a bare-breasted woman sprawled on the sidewalk with her panties pulled down. A robot/monster stood over her, while a huge flying creature with tiny red demonic-looking cling-ons hovered above. After many complaints, the rape scene was replaced by a cross with five skulls— one for each band member—but the controversial scene was printed on the inside liner.

Not only do today's songs glorify sex of every kind, they promote the myth that girls enjoy rape and violent, sadistic sex. Thus words like *shoot* and *bullets* and *gun* may refer to the action and anatomy of sex rather than murder. What do children learn from these double messages? Dr. Stuessy answers with a startling question:

> What if I were an impressionable fifteen-year-old boy today? My rock heroes have told me that sex on a date is expected and that it is a violent act. . . . My date is to be the object of my sexual cutting, slicing, and shooting. I must be very conscious of exerting my masculinity. I don't want my date, who, for all I know is "experienced," to think I'm a wimp! I will nail her to the bed and make her scream in pain! Boy, this sex stuff is great![25]

Tipper Gore responds, "Can anything be worse than being a teenage girl, having to cope with teenage boys who are psychologically primed to cut, slice, and shoot...? Yes—being a teenage girl programmed to accept it."[26]

☐ Drug and alcohol abuse. Song lyrics and personal testimonies extol the delights of chemical as well as sensual intoxication. Occasional warnings fade in the overwhelming contradiction of many rockers' drug-dazed lifestyles. Guzzling their favorite whiskey during concerts and singing about the types and techniques of drug abuse, idolized models—like pied pipers—draw children into a deadly trap of mindlessness, hysteria, sensuality, and violence.

A reporter from *The Boston Globe* asked Nikki Sixx of Motley Crüe (who flaunts his delight in drugs and Jack Daniels), "Do you ever have second thoughts about your influence on teenagers?" "No," replied the rocker, "I think we have a very positive message. It's very much an American message: Live free, express yourself, and it's up to the youth to change the world. Also, just have a good time."[27]

☐ Suicide and death. Many experts link the six thousand (and rising) anual teen suicides to "depression fueled by rock music and lyrics that glamorize sadistic violence and drug abuse, as well as suicide itself."[28] The coroner's report for nineteen-year-old John McCollum from Indio, California states, "Decedent committed suicide by shooting self in head with .22-caliber pistol while listening to devil music."[29]

John, who died wearing his stereo headphones, had been listening to power-packed suggestions such as, "suicide is the only way out," in Ozzy Osbourne's song "Suicide Solution" from the *Blizzard of Ozz.*

It was thought that the way to prevent suicide among teens was to treat depression. . . . That's a fallacy. It is not the case with these kids. Rather than being clinically depressed, these young suicide victims are impulsive, acting out fantasies. (Dr. Mark Rosenburg, 1988 Conference at the American Society of Suicidology)

□ The occult. "I like to drink blood out of a skull and torture females on stage,"[30] says W.A.S.P.'s Blackie Lawless, master of shock rock. His concert props give the appearance that he means what he says.

A small fraction of the horrendous consequences of dabbling in the occult have come into public view in recent years—stories too horrible to comprehend, like that of fourteen-year-old Tom Sullivan. In January 1988, after a classroom assignment to research different religions, Tommy became fascinated with satanism. He dreamt Satan told him to kill his family, so he murdered his mother with his Boy Scout knife, tried to burn his home, slashed his own wrists and throat, and died outside in the snow. In his diary, "Book of Shadows," he had written:

> *To the Greatest Demons of Hell I, Tommy Sullivan, would like to make a solemn exchange with you. If you give me the most extreme of all magical powers . . . I will kill many Christian followers who are serious in their beliefs . . . I will tempt all teenagers on earth to have sex, have incest, do drugs, and to worship you. I believe that evil will once again rise and conquer the love of God.*[31]

Throughout the week before the killing, Tommy, whose room was decorated with posters of his favorite heavy-metal musicians, had been singing a song "about blood and killing your mother."[32]

People are drawn in [to satanism] by music. . . . When you've got this music playing over and over again all the time—you know, Megadeth, Slayer, Metallica—and you're hearing praise to the devil and . . . to the ideals of evil, you begin to cheer for it." (Pete Roland, satanic killer.)[33]

AC/DC's Bon Scott died soon after recording *Highway to Hell.* He asphyxiated in his own vomit, joining the ranks of Jimi Hendrix and many other hard-drinking, drug-dazed rock idols.

AC/DC quickly plugged in a new lead singer, but the same mocking spirit can be heard as he shrieks out the incredibly arrogant words of "Back in Black" at jackhammer speed: "I'm let loose from the noose . . . /I got nine lives . . . running wild." Indeed he is. In "Hells Bells" he hisses, "Got my bell, I'm gonna take you to hell. . . ."[34]

"There's a battle going on and the battleground is the kids," says Doug Raley, director of Frontline Ministries in Central Oregon. "There are casualties and fatalities. . . . It's a physical and spiritual war that's as real as the Vietnam War. . . ."[35]

□ One world government. While the dark side of the occult rages openly, an equally sinister assault hides behind the bright lie of global peace. Rock 'n' roll spectaculars like "Live Aid" and "Freedomfest" joined rock idols and their billions of worshipers in worldwide celebrations of globalist visions. "We Are the World,"[36] they proclaimed, not realizing they celebrated a counterfeit oneness based on the New Age monism: All is one.

Many megastars who proclaim New Age consciousness-raising and leftist political ideologies, have been commended for their social concern. What do they teach? A popular song, "When the Children Cry" from the album, *Pride*, by White Lion typifies the same anti-American, one-world sentiment we saw in global education: "No more presidents/ And all the wars will end/One united world under God."[37]

Their god is not our God, as evidenced by *Pride's* other songs. There can be no peaceful united world until "at the name of Jesus every knee [will] bow . . . and every tongue confess that Jesus Christ is Lord" (Philippians 2:10-11). Between now and that great day, the world will be duped into welcoming a global religion and government. It will worship the ruler of the "one united world," the Antichrist, Satan's shrewd, cruel puppet (Revelation 13:8). Meanwhile, we are reminded:

> *We do not belong to the night or to the darkness. So then, let us not be like others, who are asleep, but let us be alert and self-controlled . . . putting on faith and love as a breastplate, and the hope of salvation as a helmet. (1 Thessalonians 5:5-8)*

CHAPTER SIXTEEN
What Can Parents Do About Pagan Sentiments?

The real heroes of today are the parents, trying to raise their children in an environment that seems to have grown more and more hostile to family life. Music and the media flood their children's world with glorification of drugs and violence and perversity—and there's nothing they can do about it, they're told, because of the First Amendment. . . .

I don't believe that our Founding Fathers ever intended to create a nation where the rights of pornographers would take precedence over the rights of parents, and the violent and malevolent would be given free reign to prey upon our children. (President Ronald Reagan, October 1985)

As long as America was predominantly Christian, the Holy Spirit's presence restrained occult activities. Today, as the rebellion against God intensifies, and as Christians flirt with the world and quench God's Spirit, demonic forces rush in. Many believe that the very drumbeat that mesmerizes children is also beating out a worldwide summons to the powers of darkness.

While some may reject that theory, all can agree that music has power to influence and change people. That is why, in the Psalms alone, we are encouraged more than sixty times to sing to the Lord. Singing shapes, affirms, and strengthens what we believe. It expresses the depths of our souls. Words that enter on the wings of music tend to nest in our minds—and bounce back into our thoughts whether or not we call for them.

We can battle the contemporary decadence in music by

training our children to listen to God's thoughts, to enjoy music and songs that build faith, and to base their actions on God's truth.

Step One: Listen to God, Not the World

☐ Renew your mind with truth (Romans 12:2). Continue daily Bible study—not just to gain facts, but know and hear God's heart. He will speak to those who love and follow Him (John 10:3-5; 14:21-27). Read the following Scriptures, looking for God's messages. Discuss His guidelines; they apply to music as well as other kinds of influence.

–What is God's attitude toward evil? Psalm 97:10-11; Proverbs 6:16-19; 15:9, 26; 21:4.

–What are the consequences of playing with evil? Proverbs 1:29-33; 21:16.

–How does God want me to respond to evil? Romans 13:11-14; 1 Peter 5:6-9; Psalms 1; 141:3-4; Proverbs 2; 14:7; 24:1, 21-22.

–How does He want me to live each day? Ephesians 4:17-32; 5:3-21.

☐ Avoid compromising suggestions and situations. God says, "Flee also youthful lusts" (2 Timothy 2:22, KJV). This is not easy when a whole society craves sex and violence. Not long ago, heavy metal was on the fringe of music entertainment, and few listened to it. Now in the mainstream, it flaunts violent and graphic sexual images as damaging as those found in porn shops.

"Once I became addicted to pornography," serial murderer Ted Bundy told Dr. Dobson, "I would keep looking for more potent, more explicit, more graphic kinds of materials . . . you keep craving excitement until you reach the point where the pornography goes only so far. . . ."[1]

☐ Count on what Jesus accomplished on the cross. "[Consider] yourself dead to sin but alive to God in Christ Jesus. . . . Do not offer the parts of your body to sin, as instruments of wickedness, but rather offer yourselves to God . . ." (Romans 6:11, 13).

☐ Trust and follow the Holy Spirit. When children turn

from moral absolutes to moral relativism, they become uncomfortable in God's presence. Those who have developed an appetite for immorality hide from Him. Feeling judged by His holiness, they have two choices: run or repent and receive His loving forgiveness. Most refuse to break their bondage to their sensual lifestyle. The Apostle Paul wrote to the Galatian Christians who lived in a pagan society:

> *Live by the Spirit and you will not gratify the desires of the sinful nature. For the sinful nature desires what is contrary to the Spirit, and the Spirit what is contrary to the sinful nature. They are in conflict with each other, so that you do not do what you want. . . .*
>
> *The acts of the sinful nature are obvious: sexual immorality, impurity, and debauchery; idolatry and witchcraft; hatred, discord, jealousy, fits of rage, selfish ambition, dissensions, factions, and envy; drunkenness, orgies, and the like. I warn you, as I did before, that those who live like this will not inherit the kingdom of God.*
>
> *But the fruit of the Spirit is love, joy, peace, patience, kindness, goodness, faithfulness, gentleness, and self-control. . . . Those who belong to Christ Jesus have crucified the sinful nature with its passions and desires. Since we live by the Spirit, let us keep in step with the Spirit. (Galatians 5:16-25)*

Step Two: Help Your Child Choose Enriching Music

What is good music? This subjective question has no simple answer in these days of diverse selections and divisive preferences. While you may love classical or Christian praise music, most teenagers today do not. If your child has developed an appetite for thrash metal, you may have to start the weaning process by moving a step at a time.

☐ Ask God to lead you to His choices for your family.

☐ Listen to the music your child likes. Develop an atmosphere of love, mutual respect, and acceptance. Be open, understanding, and supportive. Discuss the message of the lyrics. Ask questions such as: "Do you agree with those lyrics? Do your friends? What happens in your mind when you keep hearing the same message over and over?"

☐ Study and buy music together. Examine record jackets, read the titles. Discuss different groups. Talk about the values, attitudes, behavior, and dress promoted by Madonna and other idols. Remember that many titles deceive. For example, the band called The Church plays neo-psychedelic music about volcano suns and magic mystery tours. In his top hit album, *Faith*, George Michael sings about sex, not God. When he sang with the group Wham, his catchy tunes emphasized kinky, sadomasochistic sex. For example, "The Edge of Heaven" suggests that straps, chains, and screams make heavenly sex.

So-called New Age music didn't seem to impress the youth culture until 1988, when Enya's hit album *Watermark* blended it with a mellow form of rock. Since the door is open to new variations, watch for hypnotic and meditative sounds intended to produce altered states of consciousness. Listen for lyrics that teach New Age spirituality. But remember, New Age music is a broad umbrella that *may* even include Christian music. As God said in 1 John 4:1, "Test the spirits."

☐ Include your child in choosing music for your home. Tell why you like certain kinds of music; share the benefits you receive. Explain that biblical truth set to music delights God and builds faith and spiritual strength in us. Ask yourselves these questions:

–Does it honor or dishonor God?

–Does it encourage me to trust and follow Him?

–Does it communicate the power of God, of man, or of Satan?

–Does it focus my mind on the glory of God or the rebellious forces of Satan? (Philippians 4:8; Colossians 3:1-3)

–Does it encourage adherence to, or rebellion against God's values?

–Does it produce a craving for a form of music rather than for God?

–In concert, do listeners worship God or the musician/ singer? (Deuteronomy 5:7-8)

☐ Consider how your music lines up with your personal

goals. Ask questions such as: Do I want to be close to God? To please Him? To enjoy His peace and protection? What happens when I listen to songs that oppose truth?

Look at Paul's goal in Philippians 3:7-10. If you choose the same goal—to know Jesus, share His suffering, and live by His resurrection life—rejection and exclusion for your obedience to Christ become stepping-stones to triumph.

☐ Set limits. While you cannot monitor what your child hears and sees at a friend's house, you *can* say no to certain kinds of music in your home. Explain your concerns. Many children welcome parental boundaries as their excuse to say no to peers.

Dr. Bernard Sable, chief guidance expert for the state of Washington, commented after a rock concert in Seattle, "There's a lot you can say about the music—why it attracts the teenage crowd. The music is loud and primitive; it's insistent and strongly rhythmic. It releases in a disguised way the all too tenuously controlled, newly acquired physical impulses of the teenager."

☐ Suggest Christian alternatives. Christian rock may not be the best substitute, but it is far better than secular rock. Check the lyrics to make sure they don't distort God's Word. For up-to-date information and suggestions, ask at your local Christian bookstore or write the Menconi Ministries, P.O. Box 969, Cardiff, CA 92007.

☐ Guard against trying to please your children by providing "Christianized" versions of pagan delights. For example, adding biblical words to a raging heavy metal beat most likely makes mockery, not wholesome music. Don't be like ancient Israel, which craved the corrupt practices of their heathen neighbors. Adding idolatry to traditional worship, they became spiritually blind and morally corrupt. Enemies invaded their land, when "every man did that which was right in his own eyes" (Judges 21:25, KJV).

Step Three: Join Group Efforts toward Constructive Change

☐ Agree with other parents on limits to destructive forms of music.

☐ Ask the youth leader of your church to teach about contemporary music.

☐ Be aware of the Parents' Music Resource Center (PMRC), which alerts us to pornographic rock music, challenges us to protect our children, and promotes standards and accountability on the part of record companies and radio shows. (Parents' Music Resource Center, 1500 Arlington Blvd., Suite 300, Arlington, VA 22209)

☐ Pray together for God's guidance and victory. Be confident that He cares about your child's spiritual health even more than you do. Remember, while He calls us to join Him in His battles, the final outcome is certain: He has won the war. Continue to thank Him!

When foreign armies attacked Jerusalem, King Jehoshaphat trusted God, called the people together, acknowledged God's superior power, and praised Him for His total sufficiency.

God responded with power-filled encouragement that lifts hearts and builds faith today. Make it your own: "Do not be afraid; do not be discouraged. Go out to face them tomorrow, and the Lord will be with you."

Do you remember the rest? Jehoshaphat organized musicians to lead the procession of soldiers into battle. Then as the people sang and praised God, He accomplished the victory on their behalf. (See 2 Chronicles 20:1-22.)

SUGGESTED READING

Raising PG Kids in an X-Rated Society by Tipper Gore
Rock Concerts: A Parent's Guide by Dr. Carl S. Taylor
Media Update, a bimonthly magazine of Menconi Ministries

AFTERWORD

Ghostbusters, Teenage Mutant Ninja Turtles, Supernaturals ...An exotic collection of action figures and accessories lay scattered on the ground outside a Boston apartment. Four-year-old Jimmy, their proud owner, smiled a welcome as I stopped to watch him play.

"Which do you like best?" I asked.

"Rock-N-Roll Michaelangelo," he answered, pointing to one of the black-belted Ninja Turtles.

As we discussed Michaelangelo and the two snakes he carried as weapons, I noticed an interesting book cover.

"May I see your book?"

"Sure. It's *Nanny Noony and the Magic Spell.*"

I opened it and read a few paragraphs. "It looks like Nanny Noony put a hex on the farm," I said.

"But she didn't really do it," protested Jimmy. "She's a good witch. She just makes potions to undo bad hexes."

Jimmy's mother, who had been listening, asked me a few questions. When she learned that I was writing about the New Age, she announced that she was a Christian. But she liked spirit-guide Seth's messages better than the Bible.

She went inside and returned with three paperbacks. "Here's what I believe," she said, handing them to me. Penned by the late trance-channeler Jane Roberts, they were filled with messages from the prolific Seth, who first "spoke" to his human medium through a Ouija board.

Soon I was sitting in her living room surrounded by New Age literature: Seth material, a magazine called *Mothering,* two books about Edgar Cayce's channeled revelations, and

The Aquarian Gospel of the Christ. The last of these, written like a Bible but presenting distortions of God's truth, fills Jesus' missing years with New Age "insights"—at the feet of "higher Masters" in India, Persia, and Egypt.

What messages do these and other spirit guides like *Ramtha* (who has about 35,000 followers), *Lazaris*, Carl Jung's *Philemon*, and thousands of *Higher Selves* bring? "You can be God! Just believe in your divinity, create your own reality, and build a new world of light and love."

Jimmy's home represents the rising number of households that have opened their doors to counterfeit gods. While millions have studied Seth's teachings, thousands of amateur spiritists have learned to channel their own spirit guides. The reports of terrifying encounters with evil spirits fade in the optimism of infinite possibilities.

What should Christian families do—hide from the world's charms or get involved? If we heed God's call to pray, study His Word, love one another in Christ, and reach out to "make disciples," can we still block the spread of evil? I believe we can. We have seen the beneficial result of a joint effort to clean up television. As Elliot Miller points out in his book, *A Crash Course on the New Age*, "We have the numbers to create a 'critical mass.'"

We can show our children how to be *in* but not *of* the world. We can demonstrate God's concern for poverty, the earth's ecology, and the threat of war—but not compromise with counterfeit solutions. We can share "truth in love" with precious people like Jimmy and his mother, while we avoid their occult practices. We can be God's ambassadors in a foreign land, shining God's light in the darkness but not allowing darkness to quench His light.

> But you, dear friends, build yourselves up in your most holy faith and pray in the Holy Spirit. Keep yourselves in God's love. . . . Be merciful to those who doubt; snatch others from the fire and save them. . . . To Him who is able to keep you from falling and to present you before His glorious presence without fault and with great joy—to the only God our Savior be glory, majesty, power, and authority, through Jesus Christ our Lord, before all ages, now and forevermore! Amen" (Jude 20–25).

GLOSSARY
OF NEW AGE TERMS

Most of the following definitions express the New Age viewpoint. Those designated *occult* offer glimpses of a mythical facade for Satan's deception—an infinitely vast, evolving fairyland teeming with supernatural "helpers." There, would-be gods play with their magic trinkets, invoke mystical powers, and create the land of their dreams. Believing *they* control this imaginary "reality," they dance blindly to Satan's tunes.

As you read, keep in mind that God repeatedly tells His people to shun occult practices and to focus on the good, not evil. While the manifestations behind these occult definitions can be demonic, psychological, or a hoax, they are all abhorrent to God.

Pray for wisdom to see from His perspective. Remember His warning: "Let no one be found among you . . . who practices divination or sorcery, interprets omens, engages in withcraft, or casts spells, or who is a medium or spiritist or who consults the dead. Anyone who does these things is detestable to the Lord" (Deuteronomy 18:10-13).

ALTERED STATES OF CONSCIOUSNESS: Mental states ranging from near normal to deep trance. Induced by spiritual exercises such as meditation, guided imagery, hypnosis, or mind-altering drugs in order to relax, experience oneness with all things, connect with "Higher Self" or channel "spirit guides."

ASCENDED BEINGS: (Occult) Highly intelligent spirit entities who have reached self-realization and now communicate with humans via channeling, visualizations, Ouija boards, etc.

ASCENDED MASTERS: (Occult) Spiritual rulers who attained self-realization, then chose to reincarnate again in order to lead the world to higher consciousness, e.g., Buddha, Vishnu, Jesus.

ASTRAL BODY: (Occult) A ghostlike, ethereal "body" shaped to fit whichever physical body it indwells, but distinct and separable from it. Between incarnations it inhabits the etheric world (Hindu heaven), where it clothes the soul-mind.

ASTRAL PROJECTIONS: (Occult) Out-of-body experiences. The astral body slips out of the physical body and travels wherever it chooses.

AUTOMATIC WRITING: (Occult) A spirit entity writes a message by moving the medium's hand and pen.

AVATAR: (Hindu) A perfected deity who returns as a spiritual leader. (See Ascended Master.)

CHAKRAS: (Hindu) Seven areas of concentrated energy marking an ascending path of consciousness from the base of the spine to the top of the head. Each chakra has its own color and rate of vibration. (See Kundalini.)

CHANNEL: (Occult) A person who yields control of his body to a spirit entity while in an altered state of consciousness such as a trance. The entity (called "familiar spirit" in the Bible) then freely communicates "higher truths" to human listeners. *Syn.*: medium, trance-channel.

CHANNELING: (Occult) A seance where people communicate with spirits who teach, answer questions, describe "past lives," diagnose illnesses, etc. While hoping to invoke a "wise" ascended being, the channel may instead open the door to confusing, hostile, and demeaning spirits.

CLAIRVOYANCE and CLAIRAUDIENCE: (Occult) The ability to see and hear beyond the natural ability of the human eye and ear.

COLOR THERAPY: (Occult) Treating disorders with colors believed to have "corresponding" vibrations. For example, put patients with stomach cancer in yellow rooms, the color frequency of the stomach.

CONSCIOUSNESS: The New Age counterpart to faith. But whereas Christian faith looks to God as its object, consciousness looks to itself as its object. Thus consciousness (infinite, interconnecting living energy and intelligence, awareness of New Age "truth"—especially the divinity of Self) begets higher consciousness (self-realization, perfection).

COSMIC CHRIST: (Occult) A creative Force essential for life, which nudges evolution toward completion.

COUNTERFEIT: A fraudulent imitation of the real thing.

A COURSE IN MIRACLES: (Occult) A popular three-volume set of instructions on New Age beliefs allegedly dictated through automatic writing by an entity called "Jesus."

CRYSTALS: (Occult) The whole range of ordinary and extraordinary crystals whose vibrational frequency supposedly cleanses, heals, balances, and strengthens the body's flow of energy.

CULT: Usually refers to a group of people who validate their beliefs with their own interpretation of the Bible, which distorts the nature and teachings of Jesus Christ.

DIVINATION: (Occult) Psychic means of gaining spiritual insights and knowledge of future events: palm reading, tarot cards, numerology, astrology, I Ching, Ouija board, meditation (when communing with one's Higher Self), self-hypnosis.

DUNGEONS AND DRAGONS: An occult role-playing, fantasy game where players fight their way through dungeons and mazes, battling a hideous array of dragons and demons. Identifying with their characters, many players lose touch with reality and become obsessed with their occult powers and the violence (torture, rape, murder) required for advancement through the levels of the game.

ESOTERIC: (Occult) Mysterious, subjective information perceived by one's feelings rather than intellect; limited to the chosen few who are able to understand it.

ETHERIC: (Occult) Pertains to the invisible realm of disembodied soul-minds, intelligences, vibrational frequencies, and energy fields.

EVOLUTION: (Occult) The process of spiritual unfolding, growth, and progress until everything reaches their "original" state of perfection. (Humanist) Through the process of natural selection, simpler forms of life progress toward higher forms.

GLOBALISM: (New Age Globalism) International joint effort to pull down national boundaries, raise planetary consciousness, create a global community through a one-world government and religion, and usher in the New Age.

GUIDE: (Occult) A highly evolved spirit entity or intelligence equipped to teach, guide, protect, and help any person who invokes its presence.

GUIDED IMAGERY: Visualization exercises directed by a teacher or leader. While some merely relax, others produce altered states of consciousness including trance, a sense of astral projection, and connection with a spirit guide.

HIGHER SELF: (Occult) The God-Self, the I AM, "my inner Self." Contains all cosmic knowledge, wisdom, and power—just as each unit of a hologram contains all the characteristics of the whole.

HOLISTIC: Focuses on the whole rather than on parts. Deals with the whole person—body, soul, and spirit.

HYPNOSIS: A sleeplike state (often trance). The subject surrenders his mind and body into the hands of the hypnotist, leaving himself passive and open to all kinds of suggestions.

HYPNOTIC REGRESSION: Taking a person back into his past, including "past lives," through hypnosis. Testimonies from such regressions are widely accepted as proof of reincarnation, even though scientists have proven how easily outside suggestions can manipulate "memories."

I CHING: (Occult) Divining future events by tossing three coins six times and reading a message in the sides that face up. I Ching or Book of Changes is an ancient Chinese method of consulting an "oracle" for answers to questions, especially about decisions. The I Ching shows a person how to make his life flow smoothly with the universe.

KARMA: The Hindu and Buddhist answer to eternal justice. Each person's attitudes and actions in past lives determine his future lives. A western adaption to New Agers' denial of guilt permits some to say, "I can do what I want and not worry; if I hurt you, you had it coming."

KUNDALINI: (Hindu) A capricious force symbolized by a coiled snake resting at the base of the spinal column. Activated by yogic meditation, the Kundalini serpent uncoils and forces its way up through the seven CHAKRAS (the THIRD EYE is the sixth) until it reaches the CROWN CHAKRA, union with the Source.

LEVITATION: (Occult) To lift something into the air with psychic rather than physical power.

MANTRA: (Hindu) A word or formula (usually names or titles of Hindu gods) chanted repetitively to empty and center the mind and raise spiritual awareness. May invoke the presence of that god (a demonic ruler within Satan's hierarchy of principalities and forces which control various territories on earth. (See Daniel 10:13 and Ephesians 6:12.)

MEDITATION: (Hindu) A disciplined focus on a given mantra or theme such as Self, for the purpose of relaxing, attaining higher states of consciousness, and connecting with the cosmic mind. See KUNDALINI. The fact that there is danger in Eastern meditation must not deter us from biblical meditation. God does not ask us to passively empty our minds, but to meditate on biblical truths about Himself and His ways "day and night." (See Psalms 1:1-3 and 63:6.)

NEW AGE NETWORK: Informal ties that effectively join the innumerable interest groups that identify with New Age beliefs and goals.

NUMEROLOGY: (Occult) A form of divination based on hidden meanings in numbers, especially birth dates.

OCCULT: Hidden, secret, mysterious pursuit of supernatural powers in the practice of witchcraft, satanism, astrology, and spiritualism. Those in the occult may use the Kabbalah, Tarot Cards, and I Ching. Involves supernatural schemes and powers that oppose God's Kingdom.

ONENESS: (Hindu) The pantheistic/monistic theme that weaves through New Age idealism, especially globalism. Like love and peace, it is more readily discussed in visionary terms than practiced among individuals.

OUIJA BOARD: A popular form of divination in which people seek spiritualistic or telepathic messages. A number of people have tested the Ouija board by asking about Jesus Christ and the cross. The board's dramatic responses, ranging from violent shaking to flipping against a wall or person, demonstrate demonic hatred of Christ.

PARAPSYCHOLOGY: A field of study concerned with the investigation of evidence for paranormal psychological phenomena, such as telepathy, clairvoyance, and psychokinesis.

POLTERGEISTS: Spirits or demons who show their presence by moving visible objects or making unexplained noises such as rappings.

POLYTHEISM: Many gods, as in Greek mythology, wicca, shaamanism.

POSITIVE MENTAL ATTITUDE (PMA): Usually associated with human potential movement and the New Age belief that positive thoughts have power to manipulate circumstances, i.e., "I can create my own reality."

PSYCHIC: Using occult power to perform extrasensory feats such as clairvoyance, telepathy, divination, etc.

PSYCHIC HEALER: Someone who invokes occult power and channels this "healing energy" to others.

PSYCHOMETRY: (Occult) Receiving psychic information through the palms of the hands by touching or handling an object.

PYRAMID: Literally means "glorious light," from the Greek "pyros" which means fire. Many believe that the pyramidal shape will balance a person's energy and enhance spiritual enlightenment.

REINCARNATION: (Hindu, transmigration) Man never dies but continues life in one body after another. Whether he returns as a human or an animal depends on performance in past lives. Only perfection can free him from the miserable cycle of incarnations.

To sell their religion to Americans, guru missionaries packaged their beliefs in more positive terms: No risk of becoming a fly. Future incarnations meant evolutionary progress toward better lives.

God says, "Man is destined to die once, and after that to face judgment" (Hebrews 9:27). No one gets a second chance!

SHAMAN: A "priest" or "witch doctor" with power to channel occult power; a mediator between his tribe and the "forces of nature" or "good and evil spirits."

SPIRIT GUIDE: (Occult) A highly evolved spirit entity who enters a relationship with a medium and provides information on request.

According to Unger's Bible Dictionary, a "familiar spirit is a divining demon present in the physical body of the conjurer." It was called "familiar" because of the intimate relationship between the spirit (who could be summoned any time) and the person possessing it.

SPIRITISM: (Occult) Mediumistic activity based on the belief that the spirits of the dead and other etheric intelligences are ready and waiting to communicate with earthlings.

SPIRIT LOVER: (Occult) An etheric entity who enters into a sexual relationship with an earthling. (Consider Genesis 6:1-7)

TAROT CARDS: (Occult) Divination based on the occult symbols and meanings on each of the seventy-eight cards. For example, the TAROT KING represents Self.

THIRD EYE: (Hindu) An imagined organ (the sixth chakra) behind the "holy spot" in the forehead believed to be the center of psychic or all-seeing vision.

TRANCE: (Occult) A deep sleeplike condition which prepares the subject to be inhabited and used by higher intelligences. (See Channel)

TRANSCENDENT: Rising beyond; surpassing the physical senses. (Occult) Higher states of consciousness and levels of reality reached by spiritual exercises such as guided imagery. (See Astral Projection)

TRANSPERSONAL: Beyond objective reality. Involves altered states of consciousness and psychic or occult influences.

TRUTH: While God's truth is the body of absolute, unchangeable facts revealed in the Bible, New Age truth is subjective and personal. Since everyone is God, each person can create his own personal reality and define truth according to his personal preference and understanding.

UFO: Unidentified flying object. While most reported sightings have a natural explanation, some, especially those involving contact with extra-terrestrials, are supernatural. Christian authorities such as Walter Martin, John Weldon, and Clifford Wilson believe these to be demonic manifestations. Case studies of encounters and abductions reveal mind-manipulation (such as through hypnosis) and trance states, rather than physical displacement. "Alien" contacts are often made through occult activities like the Ouija board and yoga.

WHIRLING DERVISH: (Occult) A Muslim Leader known for whirling movements which supposedly induce higher states of consciousness and psychic experiences.

WICCA: Witchcraft or "Wise one." Employs sorcery and mystical rites for "black" or "white" magic, communion with forces of nature, and worshiping "mother earth."

YIN-YANG: (Chinese, Occult) Two opposite but complementary energies of any unified whole: positive/negative, male/female, light/dark, strong/weak. The two balancing polarities of the universal force which infuses all things. Symbolized by a circle divided by a serpentine line. Yin is the black side with the white "eye," Yang is white with a black "eye."

LEADING YOUR CHILD TO RECEIVE JESUS AS SAVIOUR AND LORD

"Unless a man is born of water and the Spirit, he cannot enter the kingdom of God. Flesh gives birth to flesh, but the Spirit gives birth to spirit. You should not be surprised at My saying, "You must be born again" (John 3:5-7).

Without God's Spirit, children cannot truly know God or understand the Bible. Born again by His Spirit, they can enjoy and exercise all the marvelous privileges of citizenship in God's wonderful kingdom (Ephesians 1:1–2:10).

How do we lead our children into an eternal love relationship with Jesus Christ?

☐ Pray that God will prepare their hearts. Spiritual rebirth is God's work, not ours (John 6:44). We merely cooperate with God's process.

☐ Lay a foundation. Include Jesus in your conversations. Let your children hear you talk to Him. Pray with them. Talk about how He helps you each day. Make comments like, "Jesus understands. He is sad when you are sad. Let's ask Jesus what He wants us to do."

☐ Wait for God's timing. While you watch for signs of openness, be ready for an opportune moment. Perhaps it will come at a time of special need for comfort and strength. Or when a child shows you by his questions that he genuinely wants to know, and follow God.

☐ Explain the basic saving truths. Lead your child through these steps, then ask if he wants to pray to receive Jesus. If he says no, tell him that he can pray that prayer anytime on his own with the same wonderful results.

If your child wants to pray alone, suggest that he come and tell you afterward. Don't forget the date. Keep it as a most special birthday.

—God loves you. He wants you to be part of His special family. He wants you to live with Him in His invisible kingdom. "Let the little children come to Me, and do not hinder them, for the kingdom of God belongs to such as these" (Luke 18:16).

—By yourself, you can't come to God. God is holy and perfect and can't let any sin into His kingdom. Sin separates us from Him (Isaiah 59:2). "For all have sinned and come short of the [perfect goodness] of God" (Romans 3:23). Think about the different kinds of sin like selfishness, envy, lying, wanting your own way. Can you be completely free from them? No you can't, no matter how hard you try.

—Jesus made a way for you. He said, "I am the way.... No one comes to the Father except through Me" (John 14:6). He died on the cross, taking the punishment for your sins. "God loved the world so much that He gave His one and only Son so that whoever believes in Him shall not perish but have eternal life" (John 3:16).

—You must invite Jesus to come and live in you. "To all who received Him, to those who believed in His name, He gave the right to become children of God" (John 1:12). With His perfect life inside, you may live and walk with God forever.

Your prayer must include confession (admit you are a sinner), repentance (turn from wrong ways and follow Jesus), faith (trust that Jesus died and rose again to save you from sin), and the invitation.

Pray something like this: "Dear Jesus, I know I have sinned and don't deserve to be Your child. But I believe that You died for me and have forgiven me. Please come into my heart. Thank you."

"When someone becomes a Christian he becomes a brand new person inside. He is not the same any more. A new life has begun." (2 Corinthians 5:17, TLB)

ENDNOTES

Chapter One

1. Information together with copies of a letter and a memorandum to Ken Roberts from the principal were distributed by Beverly LaHaye, Concerned Women of America, January 1989.

2. Therese Iknoian, "Teachers' Lesson in Self-Esteem," *San Jose Mercury News*, 12 October 1988.

3. Told by a parent in Palo Alto, California.

4. John Dunphy, "A Religion for a New Age," *The Humanist* (January/February 1983): 26.

5. *The Humanist Manifesto I* (1933)—the first public declaration of the views and objectives of humanism—rejected God and His values, but affirmed humanist faith in the power and evolution of man. *The Humanist Manifesto II* (1973) reaffirmed and amplified this man-centered, relativistic, utopian belief-system.

6. Bill Sidebottom, "This Teacher's Union Agenda Has Little to Do with Education," *Citizen* (September 1988): 10–11.

7. Paul C. Vitz, *Censorship—Evidence of Bias in Our Children's Textbooks* (Ann Arbor, Michigan: Servant Books, 1986), 3–4, 18–19.

8. Mel and Norma Gabler, *What Are They Teaching Our Children?* (Wheaton, Illinois: Victor Books, 1985), 38.

9. Deborah Rozman, *Meditating with Children* (Boulder Creek, California: University of the Trees Press, 1975), v.

10. Rozman, 32.

11. *Ibid.*, 96.

12. *Ibid.*, 42.

13. *Ibid.*, 115.

14. *Ibid.*, 146.

15. Shirley Correll, "Quieting Reflex and Guided Imagery: Education for the New Age," *Pro-Family Forum Alert* (September 1985): 5.

16. Gabler and Gabler, 39, citing *People of the World, Teacher Tactics,*

Scott Foresman Spectra Program (Scott Foresman and Company, 1975), 50.

17. Told by a high school student in Mountain View, California.

18. *Ibid.*

19. Gabler and Gabler, 39–40.

Chapter Two

1. Cyndie Huntington and Nita Scoggan, *Combat Handbook for Parents with Children in Public Schools* (Manassas, Virginia: Royalty Publishing Company, 1988), 9–10.

2. Phyllis Schlafly, *Child Abuse in the Classroom* (Westchester, Illinois: Crossway Books, 1988), 8.

3. David Schimmel and Lois Fischer, *The Rights of Parents in the Education of Their Children* (Columbia, Maryland: National Committee for Citizens in Education, 1977), 1.

Chapter Three

1. Judges 17:6 and 21:25

2. Phyllis Schlafly, *Child Abuse in the Classroom* (Westchester, Illinois: Crossway Books, 1988), 194–195.

3. *Ibid.*, 146.

4. Marilyn Ferguson, *The Aquarian Conspiracy* (New York: St. Martin's Press, 1987), 397.

5. *Ibid.*, 389.

6. *Ibid.*, 392.

7. Paul de Parrie and Mary Pride, *Unholy Sacrifices of the New Age* (Westchester, Illinois: Crossway Books, 1988), 154–155.

8. Faye Wattleton, "Reproductive Rights for a More Humane World," *The Humanist* (July/August 1986): 7.

9. William Glasser, M.D., *Schools Without Failure* (New York: Harper & Row, 1969), 161.

10. Sidney B. Simon, Leland W. Howe, and Howard Kirschenbaum, *Values Clarification—A Handbook of Practical Strategies for Teachers and Students* (New York: Hart Publishing Co., 1972), 38.

11. *Ibid.*, 39, 41–46.

12. *Ibid.*, 49, 54.

13. Schlafly, 57.

14. *Ibid.*, 45–46.

15. Richard A. Baer, Jr., "Teaching Values in the Schools," *American Education* (November 1982): 11.

16. Schlafly, 156–157.

17. *Ibid.*, 126.

18. *Ibid.*, 83–84.

19. *Ibid.*, 27.

20. *Ibid.*, 34.

21. *Ibid.*, 137.

22. Dr. Robert Simonds, *As the Twig Is Bent* (Costa Mesa, California: Citizens for Excellence in Education, 1984), 40, citing Sidney Simon, "Sexuality in School," *Colloquy* (May 1970).

23. Simon, Howe, and Kirschenbaum, 119.

24. Baer, 15.

25. Ruth Bell, *Changing Bodies, Changing Lives* (New York: Random House, 1980), 94. Cited in Jane Chastain, *I'd Speak Out on the Issues If I Only Knew What to Say.*

26. *Ibid.*, 114.

27. *Ibid.*, 121.

28. *Ibid.*, 87.

29. Elizabeth Winship, Frank Caparulo, and Vivian K. Harlin, *Masculinity and Femininity*, revised (Boston: Houghton Mifflin Co., 1978), 63.

30. *Ibid.*, 57.

31. Ferguson, 398.

Chapter Four

1. Richard A. Baer, Jr., "Teaching Values in the Schools," *American Education* (November 1982): 12.

2. Dr. Robert Simonds, "President's Report," (Costa Mesa, California: Citizens for Excellence in Education, January 1989).

Chapter Five

1. Robert Muller, *New Genesis: Shaping a Global Spirituality* (New York: Doubleday and Co., 1982), 49.

2. William M. Bowen, Jr., past president of the Capital chapter of the Christian Educators Association, is a schoolteacher and the author of *Globalism—America's Demise.*

3. Mel and Norma Gabler, *What Are They Teaching Our Children?* (Wheaton, Illinois: Victor Books), 47–48, citing:

Search for Freedom: America and Its People (The Macmillan Company, 1973), 7, 348, 384–390, 403, 412.

Many Peoples, One Nation (Random House, Inc., 1973), 88. Adapted from a speech by Frederick Douglass and presented to students in the present tense without refutation.

A Global History (Allyn and Bacon, Inc., 1979), Units 4–9.

A Global History of Man (Allyn and Bacon, Inc., 1970), 444.

*From an address by the editor of *This Week* magazine (Spring 1962).

4. Dr. James Kennedy, *Train Up a Child* (Fort Lauderdale, Florida: Coral Ridge Ministries, sermon delivered on 2 June 1985), 7.

5. Kathleen Hayes and Samantha Smith, *Grave New World* (Golden, Colorado: New Awareness Consultants, 1986), 18.

6. William Bennett, former U.S. Secretary of Education, "America, the World and Our Schools," presented at the Ethics and Public Policy Center Conference, Washington, D.C., 5 December 1986, p. 7.

7. Andre Ryerson, "The Scandal of 'Peace Education,'" *Commentary* (June 1986): 38–41.

8. Bennett, 8, 10.

9. Ken Keyes, Jr., *The Hundredth Monkey* (St. Mary, Kentucky: Vision Books, 1982), 13–18.

10. John Randolph Price, *The Planetary Commission* (Austin, Texas: The Quartus Foundation for Spiritual Research, Inc., 1984), 68–69.

11. Bennett, 9.

12. "An Emerging Coalition: Political and Religious Leaders Come Together," A Special Report, *The Omega Letter* (North Bay, Ontario, Canada, November 1988): 2.

13. *Ibid.*, 3.

14. Paul de Parrie and Mary Pride, *Unholy Sacrifices of the New Age* (Westchester, Illinois: Crossway Books, 1988), 76.

15. *Ibid.*, 75 citing Professor Richard Mitchell, *The Leaning Tower of Babel* (Boston: Little, Brown and Company), 1984.

16. *Ibid.*, 75.

17. Phyllis Schlafly, *Child Abuse in the Classroom* (Westchester, Illinois: Crossway Books, 1988), 308.

18. Education Reporter (March 1988): 1.

19. Gregg L. Cunningham, "Blowing the Whistle on 'Global Education,'" prepared for Thomas G. Tancredo, Regional Representative, U.S. Department of Education, Denver, Colorado, 1986, p. 22, citing *Death: A Part of Life* (Denver: Center for Teaching International Relations, 1981), 39.

20. *Ibid.*, 47.

Chapter Six

1. D.L. Cuddy, "Education: Globalism Tramples on American Values," *The Christian World Report* (April 1989): 12.

2. Peter Lalonde, *The Omega Letter* (May 1989): 17.

3. Hank Paulson, *Beyond the Wall* (Ventura, California: Regal Books, 1982), 76–77.

Chapter Seven

1. Donald E. Wildmon, *The Home Invaders* (Wheaton, Illinois: Victor Books, 1987), 19.

2. *Ibid.*, 22.

3. *Ibid.*, 23.

4. Marilyn Ferguson, *The Aquarian Conspiracy* (Los Angeles: J.P. Tarcher, Inc., 1980), 49.

5. Patrick Buchanan, "Hollywood's War on Christianity," *San Jose Mercury News*, 28 July 1988.

6. *Ibid.*

7. David Ansen, "The Raider of Lost Art," *Newsweek* (23 May 1988): 70.

8. "What's News," *Media Update*, Menconi Ministries (November/December 1988): 10.

Chapter Eight

1. Marlin Maddoux, *American Betrayed* (Lafayette, Louisiana: Huntington House, Inc., 1984), 92.

Chapter Nine

1. Donald E. Wildmon, *The Home Invaders* (Wheaton, Illinois: Victor Books, 1987), 93.

2. *Ibid.*

3. Paula Patyk, *Parental Adviser* (Knoxville, Tennessee: Whittle Communications, 1987), 2.

4. Wilson Bryan Key, *Subliminal Seduction* (New York: NAL Penguin, Inc.), 67–68.

5. Marlin Maddoux, *America Betrayed* (Shreveport, Louisiana: Huntington House, Inc., 1984), 87.

6. NBC TV, Saturday morning, 25 March 1989.

7. Maddoux, 39–40.

8. Peter Lalonde, *The Omega Letter*, October 1988, 16.

9. Jim Trelease, *The Read-Aloud Handbook* (New York: Penguin Books), 93.

10. Phil Phillips, *Turmoil in the Toybox* (Lancaster, Pennsylvania: Starburst Publisher, 1986), 49.

11. Michalene Busico, "TV or not TV," *San Jose Mercury News*, 13 December 1988.

12. Ellen Creager, "Studying the Effects of Screen Sex on Teens," *San Jose Mercury News*, 12 March 1989.

13. Paula Patyk, *Parental Adviser* (Knoxville, Tennessee: Whittle Communications, 1987), 2.

14. Phillips, 49.

15. Complete tape messages available from *Focus on the Family*, Pomona, California 91799.

16. Wildmon, 77.

Chapter Ten

1. Jane Chastain, *I'd Speak Out on the Issues If I Only Knew What to*

Say (Ventura, California: Regal Books, 1987), 182.

2. Paula Patyk, *Parental Adviser* (Knoxville, Tennessee: Whittle Communications, 1987), 2.

3. Frank York, "Homemaker Takes on Fox Television," *Citizen* (April 1989): 12.

4. Donald E. Wildmon, *The Home Invaders* (Wheaton, Illinois: Victor Books, 1987), 9.

5. *Intercessors for America Newsletter,* Reston, Virginia, October 1988.

Chapter Eleven

1. "Notes and Quotes," *Frontpage,* A Publication of Today, the Bible and You (July 1988): 5.

2. *Topeka Capital—Journal* (9 February 1985), quoted in *Pro-Family Alert* (April 1985): 2.

3. Rence Melton, "Fantasy Game Can Turn Demonic," *The Bend Bulletin* [Oregon], 9 October 1988.

4. Larry McLain, from tape of lecture titled, "The Rising Interest in the Supernatural" given at the Seventh Mid-America Prophecy Conference, Oklahoma City, 27 July 1988.

Chapter Twelve

1. Joanne Oppenheim, *Buy Me, Buy Me* (New York: Pantheon Books, 1987), 14.

2. Francie Scott, "Gospel According to Barbie," *Christian Home* (Winter 1984–85): 21.

3. *Ibid.*

4. Oppenheim, 23.

Chapter Thirteen

1. "What Next," *Sassy* (July 1988): 20.

2. "Watch It," *Sassy* (July 1988): 22.

3. Christina Kelly, "What Now?" *Sassy* (July 1988): 14.

4. *Webster's Third New Unabridged Dictionary,* 1965.

5. J.D. Reed, "Packaging the Facts of Life," *Time* (August 1982): 65.

6. Judy Blume, *Forever* (New York: Pocket Books, 1975), 129.

7. Book Reviews, "Arts and Books," *San Jose Mercury News,* 27 November 1988.

8. Michael Pappas, *Sweet Dreams for Little Ones* (San Francisco: Harper and Row, 1982), 48.

9. Paul A. Bartz

10. Francis Hodgson Burnett, *The Secret Garden* (New York, Henry Holt and Company, 1987), 187, 190.

11. *Ibid.,* 188.

12. *Ibid.*, 187.
13. *Ibid.*, 190.
14. Rose Estes, *Dragon of Doom*, A Dungeons & Dragons Adventure Book (Lake Geneva, Wisconsin: TSR, Inc., 1983), 84.
15. Dr. Seuss, *The Butter Battle Book* (New York: Random House, 1984), 6.
16. *Ibid.*

Chapter Fourteen

1. McInerney, *Bright Lights, Big City* (New York: Vintage Contemporaries, 1984), 6–7.
2. Neil Postman, *Amusing Ourselves to Death* (New York: Viking Penguin, Inc., 1985), vii-viii.
3. Jim Trelease, *The Read-Aloud Handbook* (New York: Penguin, 1987), 40.
4. *Seventeen*, January 1989, pp. 92, 82, 12.
5. "X-Rated Children's Books," (ProFamily Forum, P.O. Box 8907, Fort Worth, Texas 76124).

Chapter Fifteen

1. "The Power of the Young," "Star Rap" column, *Faces Magazine* (19 September 1984): 50.
2. Robin Richman, "An Infinity of Jimi," *Life* (3 October 1969): 4.
3. Nevill Drury, *Music for Inner Space* (Dorset, California: Prism Press, 1985), 21.
4. *Ibid.*, 28.
5. Kathleen Donnely, "Giving Voice to the Magic of Africa's Talking Drums," *San Jose Mercury News*, 7 April 1989.
6. Drury, 18, citing A.J. Langguth, *Macumba*, 1975, 70.
7. Manfred Clynes (ed.), *Music, Mind and Brain* (New York: Plenum Publishing Corporation, 1982), 174.
8. Drury, 18.
9. Jeff Lilley, "Dabbling in Danger," *Moody Monthly* (March 1989): 17.
10. Dave Hart, *Heavy Metal Madness* (Cardiff, California: Menconi Ministries, 1989), 3.
11. Lilley, 3.
12. Hart, 2.
13. Ozzy Osbourne, "No Bone Movies," *Blizzard of Ozz*, Jet Music Ltd., CBS, 1981.
14. Venom, "Sacrifice," *Here Lies Venom*, Neat Music, Combat Records MX8062. Written by Dunn, Bray, Lant. Cited in Tipper Gore, *Raising PG Kids in an X-Rated Society* (Nashville: Abingdon Press, 1987), 120.
15. "Rock 'n' Roll's Leading Lady," *Time* (16 December 1974): 63.
16. *Rock and Roll: A Search for God*, video cassette with Eric Holmberg, Reel to Real Ministries, P.O. Box 44290, Pittsburgh, PA 15205, quoting

Angus Young, *Hit Parade*, July 1985, 60.

17. *Rising to the Challenge*, an educational video presentation, Parents' Music Resource Center, Arlington, Virginia, 1988.

18. Peggy Mann, "How Shock Rock Harms Our Kids," *Reader's Digest* (July 1988): 102.

19. *Ibid.*, 102.

20. Venom, *Welcome to Hell*, Combat Records, 1985.

21. *Rock and Roll: A Search for God*, quoting Bay Area Magazine, 1 February 1977.

22. Poison, *Open Up and Say Ah*, Capitol Records.

23. Prince, "Sister," *Dirty Mind*, Warner Brothers Records, 1980.

24. Lyrics included in Guns N' Roses, *Appetite for Destruction*, Geffen Records, Warner Brothers Communication Co., 1987.

25. Gore, 89.

26. *Ibid.*, 90,

27. *Ibid.*, 149.

28. Mann, 103.

29. *Ibid.*

30. Gore, 47, citing "An Exclusive Talk with a Shocking Performer—Blackie Lawless," *RockLine* (April 1985): 14.

31. Jeff Lilley, "Evil in the Land," *Moody Monthly* (March 1989): 14.

32. "Boy Became Killer After Occult Interest," *San Jose Mercury News*, 13 January 1988.

33. *Geraldo*, August 14, 1989.

34. AC/DC, *Back in Black*, Atlantic Recording Corporation, Warner Communications Co., 1980.

35. Renoe Melton, "Icons of Satanism Lurk in Records, Films, Television," *Bend Bulletin* [Oregon], 9 October 1988.

36. By Lionel Ritchie and Michael Jackson.

37. White Lion, *Pride*, Double Trouble Productions, Inc., 1987.

Chapter Sixteen

1. "Ted Bundy's Death-Row Message: Pornography Is a Fatal Addiction," *Citizen* (March 1989): 15.